GW00673122

SLIPPING THE LEG (AFTER ALFIERI, 1640).

[*Frontispiece.*]

The line A gives the alternative of a cut inside the face, and the line B that of a cut outside the arm.

THE SWORDSMAN

A Manual of Fence

FOR THE

FOIL, SABRE, AND BAYONET.

BY

ALFRED HUTTON, F.S.A.

Late Captain King's Dragoon Guards;

AUTHOR OF "COLD STEEL," "FIXED BAYONETS," ETC.

With Forty-two Illustrations.

NEW AND CHEAPER EDITION.
WITH AN APPENDIX
THE GRIPS AND CLOSES,

The Naval & Military Press Ltd

published in association with

ROYAL
ARMOURIES

Published by the
The Naval & Military Press
in association with the Royal Armouries

Unit 10 Ridgewood Industrial Park,
Uckfield, East Sussex, TN22 5QE
Tel: +44 (0) 1825 749494
Fax: +44 (0) 1825 765701

For a full listing of all N&MP titles, visit:
www.naval-military-press.com

MILITARY HISTORY AT YOUR FINGERTIPS

Online genealogy research:
www.military-genealogy.com

ROYAL
ARMOURIES

The Library & Archives Department at the Royal Armouries Museum, Leeds, specialises in the history and development of armour and weapons from earliest times to the present day. Material relating to the development of artillery and modern fortifications is held at the Royal Armouries Museum, Fort Nelson.

For further information contact:
Royal Armouries Museum, Library, Armouries Drive,
Leeds, West Yorkshire LS10 1LT
Royal Armouries, Library, Fort Nelson, Down End Road, Fareham PO17 6AN

Or visit the Museum s website at
www.armouries.org.uk

In reprinting in facsimile from the original, any imperfections are inevitably reproduced and the quality may fall short of modern type and cartographic standards.

Printed and bound by CPI Antony Rowe, Eastbourne

To

LIEUT.-COLONEL H. C. CHOLMONDELEY

AND

THE MEMBERS OF THE SCHOOL OF ARMS

OF THE

LONDON RIFLE BRIGADE.

CONTENTS.

PART I.

THE FOIL.

PART II.

THE SINGLESTICK AND SABRE.

PART III

THE BAYONET.

INTRODUCTION.

IF this little book should in any way assist in rescuing the Art of Fence in this country from the debased state into which of late years it has fallen, owing, I fear, mainly to the extremely faulty and incomplete training which has for more than a quarter of a century prevailed in certain English circles, the "Swordsman" will have fulfilled his mission.

My present volume is not intended to be an elaborate treatise, but merely a handy Manual for the guidance of both teacher and pupil, demonstrating the more simple movements of attack, combined with as much variety of defence as possible; together with the most rapid method of training the sword-hand in parry and riposte. With a view to this latter I have incorporated, as an integral part of my curriculum of foil fencing, those defensive lessons performed by the pupil *with his eyes shut* which I have already recorded in the appendix to "Cold Steel." Mr. Colmore Dunn, the author of one of the very best of the minor works on our subject, alludes to these as "an interesting experiment." Interesting they certainly are; but the experimental stage is one which they have long passed. They were imparted to me many years ago by the greatest swordsman and the most accomplished master of the art that the British nation has ever produced—the late Mr. McTurk, who was for a long period of time the head of Messrs. Angelo's School of Arms in St. James's Street, and who had in his turn received them from the last of the Angelos himself. They are of such marvellous efficacy in rapidly training the hand and in imparting to it that delicate sense of touch known to the French as *sentiment du fer*, that I have decided to insert them in this little book, in such a manner as will, I hope, make it quite clear that they are to form part of the regular course of instruction.   I do not think that these *Blindfold Lessons* could well be adapted to the military system of fencing as now taught in the army, the defensive movements which the instructors are compelled to teach being, to my mind, of much too clumsy a nature.

With regard to the parries, which are eight in number, I have selected for use those four which are formed with the hand in "supination," or with the palm upwards; for when the palm is turned down the action of the biceps muscle ceases to a great extent, and thus the hand is liable to be drawn downwards into positions from which it is very difficult to recover it.

In compiling the part of this book devoted to the foil, I have consulted largely the French military "Manuel d'Escrime," together with the works of Gomard, Grisier, Cordelois, and Desmedt, with an occasional glance at other authors ; while the parts relating to the sabre and to the bayonet are based on my own former works "Cold Steel" and "Fixed Bayonets."

I commence the book with the lessons on foil play, because the closeness of its movements and the delicacy of hand required in its execution render it a necessary foundation on which to base all other varieties of fence. Indeed, a man who has been reasonably well instructed in the use of the foil is able in a very short space of time to acquire facility with any other form of hand weapon that choice or necessity may cause him to select.

ALFRED HUTTON.

PART I.—THE FOIL.

PART I.

THE FOIL.

———◆———

THE foil bears the same relation to the small-sword, the duelling weapon of the French, that the singlestick does to the broadsword, being the weapon used in the fencing-room as a substitute for it both in lessons and in loose play, and it is used for striking with the point only.

Like all swords, the foil consists of two main parts—the blade and the hilt. The blade, which is nearly square, is divided into four parts: first, the "tang," or the thin roughly shaped piece of soft iron on to which the hilt is fixed; second, the "forte," that part of the blade which extends from the hilt to the centre, and with it, and it only, all thrusts made by the opponent must be turned aside; third, the "feeble," or the half extending from the centre to the point; and, fourth, the "button," the small circular steel plate which forms the point, and which it is customary to cover with a piece of parchment or leather.

The hilt is in three parts: first, the "guard," "shell," or "*lunette*," which consists of a double loop of metal, between the loops of which there is a square orifice for the tang to pass through: second, the "grip," or handle, the section of which is, like that of the blade, slightly oblong; it is about five inches in length, and is covered with string to prevent the hand from slipping; a good grip is always slightly curved, so that it may rest comfortably in the hand : third, the "pummel," which is the block of iron placed at the extreme end of the hilt, with the object of giving a proper balance to the weapon; the tang is passed through it, and is afterwards firmly riveted ; the balance of the foil should be on the blade, just above the guard.

To Change a Blade.

Supposing a blade to have been broken, which is often the case, it will be necessary to take out the broken stump and to replace it with a new blade. To effect this, place the pummel (having first wrapped a piece of stout leather round it to prevent its being damaged) in a vice, the rest of the foil being downwards. File off the rivet, and drive the tang through with the assistance of a fine-pointed punch ; and this done, the grip and guard are easily removed.

To mount the new blade.—It will be seen that all good blades are, like the best grips, slightly oblong in their section, and therefore they must be put together in such a manner that their forms shall correspond exactly, and the tang, which is purposely made of very soft metal, must be bent so as to conform to the curve of the grip, and must further be set very slightly to the left. The blade is now ready for mounting, and must be placed in the vice point downwards, close to the square shoulder from which the tang springs ; the guard must next be fitted on in such a fashion that the two loops shall correspond with the broad sides of the blade, and if it is at all loose it must be wedged up with little chips of hard wood, and the leather washer, if used, must be placed upon it ; the grip must now be very carefully put in its place, similarly wedged tight with bits of wood and hammered well home, and for this purpose a steel cylinder about eleven inches long with a hole drilled through it to admit the tang is generally used ; the pummel must be fitted on in like manner, and the protruding end of the tang must be sufficiently shortened and then hammered down into a strong rivet ; the steel button must be covered with either parchment or leather, and the foil will be ready for use.

How to Hold the Foil.

Take the foil between the forefinger and thumb of the right hand, about half an inch below the guard, the thumb to be placed on the convex side of the grip, while the concave side will rest on the middle phalange of the finger, which will be somewhat bent ; the other three fingers must rest on the grip *without pressure*, simply for the purpose of steadying it. The movements of the foil must be effected by the forefinger and thumb rather than by the wrist, and this is known as "*doigté*," or finger action.

First Position.

The pupil will place himself opposite to the master, standing erect, with his heels together, the right heel being immediately in front of the left, the right toe pointing direct to the front, and the left toe to the left; the body must be turned on the hips, so as to face about two-thirds to the front. Many masters make their pupils throw the left shoulder as far back as possible, in order to present a "feather edge" to the opponent ; this often causes the knee to be drawn inwards, and as the toe naturally follows it, the foot when moved forward on the "lunge" verges from the direct line towards the left, rendering the position both unsteady and uncouth. In cases where the pupil is slightly

Fig. 1.

in-kneed it becomes needful in the elementary lessons to counterbalance this natural defect by bringing the body still more square to the front. The left arm must hang easily at the side with the hand open ; the sword-arm must also be lowered, and quite extended a little in front of the body, with the point of the foil about four or five inches from the ground. (Fig. 1.)

The master will assume a similar position with his right foot immediately opposite to the right foot of the pupil, so that his left heel and right foot and the right foot and left heel of the pupil are all four in one straight line ; and this line is known as the " *Line of Direction.*"

To Salute.

From the first position.

1. Bend the sword-arm, bringing the elbow close to the body, with the hand on a level with the chin, and the palm turned inwards towards the face.

2. Lower the foil, and extend the arm, bringing it to the outer side of the thigh, with the palm upwards, and the point about four or five inches from the ground.

The Guard.

A "guard" is that position of person and weapon which is at once the most secure for defence and the most handy for attack.

Fig. 2.

To Come "On Guard" in Six Movements.

1. Raise the right arm until the hand reaches the height of the eyes, the arm to be completely extended, and the foil exactly in line with it, the thumb being uppermost (Fig. 2).

2. Lower the right arm to the first position (Fig. 2).

3. Turn the back of the hand up, and bring the foil to a horizontal position at the left side, the point being to the

rear, and the hilt close to the body ; the left hand must now be turned with the palm upwards, and the points of the fingers touching the guard of the foil, the blade of which must be underneath them (Fig. 3).

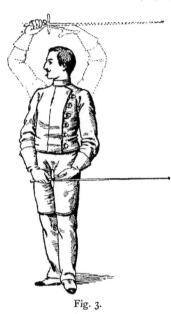

Fig. 3.

4. Raise the foil, by bending the arms and passing them upwards close to the body, until it is in a horizontal position over the head, the left hand being now underneath it (Fig. 3).

5. Lower the sword-arm to the front, the elbow to be about in line with the waist, and four or five inches in front of it, the forearm, hand, and blade to form one line, the point of the foil being about the height of the lower part of the face ; the left hand must now be at about the height of the top of the head, and the arm, hand, and fingers must form one continuous curve (Fig. 4.)

6. Bend both knees well, and advance the right foot, with a little stamp, on the line of direction, so that there shall be a space twice the length of the sole of the foot between the two heels ; the weight of the body must rest equally on both legs. This is the " *medium* guard " (Fig. 5).

To Engage

is to join and cross the blades after coming on guard.

Fig. 4.

To Advance.

Advancing, or "gaining ground," is effected in two ways, of which the first is the most usual.

1st. Step forward a short pace of not more than six inches with the right foot, and bring the left foot after it into the position of guard.

2nd. Bring the left heel completely up to the right heel,

and then step forward with the right foot into the position of guard.

This latter is extremely useful against a timid fencer, who is given to running back when attacked ; it must, however, be used with caution.

Fig. 5.

To Retire.

Retiring, or " breaking ground," is effected in three ways, of which the first is the most usual.

1st. Step back a short pace with the left foot, following it with the right.

2nd. Draw back the right foot until the heel touches the

left heel, and then step back two soles'-length with the left foot.

3rd. Spring backwards as far as you can from both feet at once, without in any way altering the distance between them.

THE APPEL.

The appel is a sharp beat or stamp given with the right foot, which in the more pedantic age of the art was greatly advocated by many of the masters.

It is of some slight use in testing the temperament of a strange opponent, as it often causes a nervous man to start back ; but where he is not of a nervous disposition this same appel will tend to rouse him, when without it he might have been caught off his guard.

The double appel consists of two consecutive beats, the first given with the heel, and the second with the sole of the foot.

THE EXTENSION OR THRUST.

At the command "Straight arm" advance the sword-hand with the palm upwards, until the arm is perfectly straight, but not rigid : the hand must be an inch or two above the level of the shoulder, and the point of the foil must be as much below that of the hand. This must be done as rapidly as possible, but *without any shock*, and without the slightest movement of body or head, and the word of command must be given quietly, and not in that jerky manner which military instructors regard as smart : jerky words of command are the direct cause of jerky action. (Fig. 6.)

Previous to instructing his pupil in the movements of the "lunge" and "recovery," the master should carefully

explain to him the object of lowering and raising the left
arm, and he should demonstrate practically how the sudden
dropping of this arm gives an initial impetus to the forward
movement, and how the velocity of the recovery is enhanced
by sharply raising it again.

Fig. 6.

THE LUNGE.

The pupil must now be taught to complete his attack
by means of the lunge, which is effected by stepping forward
with the right foot two soles'-length beyond the position
of guard. In doing so the foot must be raised as little as
possible, and must move close to the ground during its
passage ; the left arm must be quickly dropped, the palm

of the hand turned up, and the arm extended close above the left leg ; the left leg must now be quite straight, the hip must be well pressed down in order to bring the body perfectly upright, and 'the sole of the left foot must be flat on the ground ; the lower part of the right leg must be quite perpendicular, and the eyes must be fixed on the point of the foil. The complete extension of the arm must always precede the movement of the foot. (Fig. 7.)

, Fig. 7.

THE RECOVERY.

At the command " On guard" swing the left arm up ; and spring back again to the position of " guard."

The pupil must be taught to execute these two movements at first slowly, and *by degrees* to attain the utmost velocity of which he is capable.

2

Distance,

or " measure," is the exact space taken in a straight line between the combatants which must be traversed by the lunge.

Perfect measure is when you can touch the opponent by means of the lunge, without moving the left foot.

Out of measure is when it is necessary to advance in order to be near enough to touch.

Within measure is when you are so near that you can touch or be touched without lunging.

Corps à corps is when the combatants have come so close together that it is possible for them to grapple with each other.

The Target.

In foil fencing it is customary, in order to enhance precision and closeness of play, to count only those hits which strike on the chest. The "target" therefore to be aimed at is bounded horizontally by the lower edge of the collar-bone and the line of the waist, and perpendicularly by a line dropping from the front part of the armpit, and another which passes over the left nipple ; but when the combatant places himself so as to efface the whole or part of the target, the hits must count on the part which his position offers.

The Lines of Defence.

When " on guard," as before described, the foil presents two sides, that on the left of the blade being known as the " inside," and that on the right of it as the " outside ; " and these sides are again divided horizontally into " high " and " low," the parts above the guard of the foil being called "high lines," and those under it "low lines." We have, therefore, on the left of the blade, the "high inside line" and the "low inside line," and on the right of it the "high outside" and the "low outside."

These lines, as will afterwards become apparent, are also known by the names of the "guards" and of the "parries" which cover or defend them (Fig. 8).

COVERING.

The "Guards" of "Quarte" and "Sixte."

The guard which we have hitherto studied is known as the "medium guard," and it is useful mainly in the elementary lessons; but when these have been mastered we practically discard it. It will be observed that when the foil is held in this position we are open to be attacked by a simple straight thrust in any one of the four lines just described; we must therefore learn to diminish this danger by "covering" or blocking one or other of them.

Fig. 8.

To cover the "high inside line," turn the palm of the hand somewhat up, and carry the hand just enough to the left to prevent the opponent from touching with a straight thrust. Our point must now be in line with the right side of the opponent's face; this position is termed the guard in *quarte*, and the line which it covers is spoken of as the quarte line.

To cover the " high outside line," turn the palm of the hand up, and carry the hand just enough to the right to prevent the opponent from making the straight thrust, taking care not to allow the elbow to be borne to the right, but keeping it well behind the hilt. The point must now be opposite the left side of the opponent's face ; this position is termed the guard in *sixte*, and the line is called the sixte line.

SUPINATION AND PRONATION.

These two words refer only to the position in which the sword-hand is held.

When the palm is held upwards it is said to be in *supination*, and in *pronation* when turned downwards. In foil fencing I prefer the former, as in it the forearm is fully supported by the biceps muscle ; whereas when the palm is turned down it loses that support almost entirely.

OPPOSITION.

In effecting the lunge, as we have hitherto studied it, it is possible for the opponent to touch us at the same time with a counter hit by merely straightening his arm, and this we must avoid by making use of what is termed " opposition."

When, therefore, we make the attack in the quarte line, we must, during the lunge, cover our own " high inside " by carrying our hand just enough to the left to prevent the enemy's point from touching, the palm of our hand being kept well up ; and when attacking the sixte line we must carry the hand similarly a little to our right.

CHANGE OF LINE.

To change the line of engagement from quarte to sixte, pass the point underneath and close to the opponent's " forte," and assume the guard in sixte. The change from sixte to quarte is effected in a like manner.

DIRECT ATTACKS.

A direct attack is that which is made at some opening left by the opponent, and its success depends entirely on the velocity with which it is delivered. · There are four direct attacks only.

First, the straight thrust, which can only be effected when the opponent leaves open the line in which he is engaged.

The other three direct attacks are made when the opponent covers one line, upon one of the three which remain open ; and this is done by the movements known as the " disengagement," the " derobement," and the " cut over."

THE DISENGAGEMENT.

We are engaged in quarte, and the opponent's quarte line is covered, but not so his opposite sixte line ; we therefore pass our point (by " finger-action ") underneath and as close as possible to his " forte," and bring it up again into the sixte line, extending the arm completely in so doing.

Commands : " Disengage," " Lunge," " On guard."

Change to sixte, and attack the quarte line in a similar manner.

It will thus be seen that the disengagement is a direct attack on the uncovered line opposite to that on which we are engaged.

When the engagement is formed on a low line, the disengagement is made over the blade instead of under it, and the attack is made on the opposite low line.

THE DEROBEMENT.

The derobement is an attack made on the uncovered line, either high or low, on the side on which the engagement is formed.

We are engaged in quarte (inside high), and therefore the low inside is uncovered ; we lower the point, without letting the hand move downwards, and straighten the arm upon the *low inside.*

Commands : " Derobe," " Lunge," " On guard."

Change to sixte, and attack the " low outside " in the same manner.

THE CUT OVER.

This, like the disengagement, is an attack on the opposite high line, but it can only be made when the opponent makes the mistake of carrying his point too high.

Being engaged in quarte, we raise the blade with the action of the forefinger and thumb (without moving either elbow or shoulder), and pass it over the opponent's point into the sixte line, extending the arm in so doing.

Commands: " Cut over," " Lunge," " On Guard."

Change to sixte, and execute the cut over to the inside line.

THE SIMPLE PARRIES.

A parry or parade is the action of stopping or turning aside the adverse blade when it attacks.

The *simple* parry meets the opponent's blade, in the line on which the attack is made, with a little crisp, dry rap which drives its point out of line ; it is what the French call

parade du tac, and it is known only by its numerical
name. The parry by "opposition" is made by passing the
hand into the form of the parry, so as to cause the enemy's
point to glide off the forte.

Each of the four lines can be defended by two simple
parries, the first and most important being with the hand in
"supination," and the second with the hand in "pronation."

The parries in supination are the best suited for the
purposes of foil play, as in forming them the forearm is
supported by the full power of the
biceps muscle, and the hand is
therefore less likely to be drawn
downwards into a position difficult
to recover from than when the parries in pronation are used: the latter
are more suited to certain exigences of sabre work.

Fig. 9.—Medium Guard.

The parries in supination are :—

Quarte, which defends the "high inside" by turning the

Fig. 10.

palm of the hand a little up and
carrying the hand sufficiently to
the left to prevent the hostile
weapon from touching; the point
must be kept in line with the opponent's face (Fig. 10).

Sixte, which defends the "high outside" by turning the
palm up and carrying the hand
(but not the elbow) a little to the
right, keeping the point well in line
(Fig. 11).

Fig. 11.

Septime, which defends the "low
inside" by lowering the point to
about the level of the opponent's groin (taking care not to
permit the hand to sink with it), turning the palm a little

up as in quarte, and carrying the hand just enough to the

Fig. 12.

left to drive the enemy's point clear (Fig. 12).

Octave, which defends the "low outside" by lowering the point to the level of the opponent's groin, and carrying the hand with the palm upwards slightly to the right (Fig. 13).

To these four parries I shall adhere throughout the ensuing lessons.

The master cannot be too particular in insisting that on the completion of the parry the pupil's point shall not in any way be deflected from the direct line.

In teaching the parries, and, in fact, in any lesson where the lunge is not required, it is better to cause

Fig. 13.

the pupil to place his left hand on his hip, in order to avoid needless fatigue.

The attack by a *disengagement* is naturally parried in the line on which it is directed—thus : we are engaged in quarte ;

Fig. 14.

I disengage, and you parry me with sixte ; but it must be observed that in order to reach the sixte line my point has to traverse the two lower lines ; you can therefore vary your defence by stopping me half-way with septime.

Similarly, if we are engaged in septime, you can arrest my disengagement with quarte, thereby keeping me what is termed "captive" on the inner lines.

The parries in pronation are :—

Prime, which defends the "high inside" by turning the thumb downwards, with the palm of the hand to the front, and carrying the hand across the body to the left, so as to look at the enemy over the wrist. The point of the foil must be lower than the hilt, and must menace the lower lines (Fig. 14).

Fig. 15.

Tierce, which defends the "high outside" by turning the palm down and carrying the hand to the right (Fig. 15).

Fig. 16.

Quinte, which defends the "low inside" by turning the palm half down and carrying the hand a little to the left (Fig. 16).

This is the least perfect of all the simple parries, as in forming it the point naturally diverges from the direct line.

Seconde, which defends the "low outside" by turning the palm down, dropping the point to the level of the opponent's groin, and carrying the hand to the right (Fig. 17).

The Riposte.

Fig. 17.

The riposte is a return hit made immediately after parrying the attack of the opponent; and it is in order to ensure an instantaneous riposte that we are so particular about keeping the point in line during the execution of the parry. It is most effective when made from the position of guard, without moving the right foot, and it must be made with such velocity as to strike the enemy before he has commenced recovering from his lunge; but should he have commenced to recover it must be supported by the lunge, so as to touch him before he has settled himself on his guard.

The riposte, like the initial attack, must always be made with " opposition."

The pupil should be well practised in the riposte from all the four parries in supination.

THE COUNTER-RIPOSTE

is the responding attack made after having successfully parried the riposte.

THE BLINDFOLD LESSONS.—I.

THE master must now carry his pupil on to those " blind-fold lessons " which I have already recorded in " Cold Steel," and he must thoroughly understand that they are to form part of the regular instruction of *every* pupil.

The blindfold lessons to be used at this point affect the simple parries and their ripostes only ; further on I shall devote other chapters to their more varied forms. The essence of these lessons is that the pupil is taught in executing his parries and ripostes to be guided by the sense of touch alone, for during the whole of them he has his eyes shut, the result of which is that the entire power of sensibility centres itself in the arm and hand to such an extent that the nerves seem almost as if they were continued into the blade itself, the sensation of contact with the master's foil being of a magnetic nature, as if a very delicate continuous current of electricity were passing up the arm. At the instant, therefore, when this feeling ceases the pupil knows that it is time to execute the parry or series of parries which has been previously explained to him. The master will place himself at half distance, so that the pupil, after having parried, can touch with the riposte without the necessity of lunging; he will cause him to cover completely the line on which he is engaged, and will explain to him that when he perceives the contact of the blades to have ceased, he must pass his hand to the parry ordered, and so find the blade again, the master having quitted the contact in order to disengage or otherwise change his line.

When the weapons are engaged the pupil will close his eyes, and the master will *feel* the pupil's blade strongly, *not* by pressure, but by moving his own foil up and down against the centre of it, making the steel "bite;" this is what causes the magnetic sensation which I have above described. He will then direct :—

Engage my blade in quarte—cover the line—shut your eyes.

On my disengagement pass your hand to sixte, and, if you find me, riposte. On guard.

Cover yourself in sixte—I disengage, pass your hand to quarte, and, if you find me, riposte. On guard.

Cover yourself in quarte—I disengage, drop your point to septime, and, if you find me, riposte. On guard.

Engage my blade in sixte—I disengage, drop your point to octave, and, if you find me, riposte. On guard.

These movements must be continued until the pupil's hand moves readily from one position to the other, finding the blade each time and riposting instantly.

FEINTS.

Attacks in Two Movements.

A feint is a false attack made for the purpose of deceiving or decoying the opponent's blade away from the line on which the true attack is to be delivered; as he answers to the feint by parrying, the blade must be conducted to the line of the attack really intended, before he is able to find it with his parry.

Whether the feint consists of one movement or more than one, the arm must be entirely straightened on the completion of the first, and all subsequent movements must be made with it fully extended.

In all these movements the foil must be guided by finger-action, and principally by that of the forefinger.

In recording the set lessons I shall adopt the plan I have already used in " Cold Steel " and " Fixed Bayonets," of designating the master as M. and the pupil as P.   I shall commence all the lessons on the engagement in quarte, changing to others when it is necessary.

SIMPLE PARRIES DECEIVED.

Thrust and disengage, to deceive quarte and attack the sixte line.

M.	P.
Engage in quarte medium.	Straight arm.
Parry quarte.	Disengage into sixte, and lunge.

Thrust and derobe, to deceive quarte and attack the septime line.

M.	P.
Engage in quarte medium.	Straight arm.
Parry quarte.	Derobe into septime, and lunge.

Thrust and cutover, to deceive quarte and attack the sixte line.

M.	P.
Engage in quarte medium.	Straight arm.
Parry quarte.	Cut over into sixte, and lunge.

Change to sixte, and execute the above movements from that line, the master engaging in sixte medium.

One, two, to deceive sixte and attack in the quarte line.

M.	P.
Engage in quarte.	Disengage.
Parry sixte.	Disengage back again into quarte, and lunge.

The same from the sixte engagement.

Disengage and derobe, to deceive sixte and attack the octave line.

M.	P.
Engage in quarte.	Disengage.
Parry sixte.	Derobe into octave line, and lunge.

The same from the sixte engagement.

Under and over, to deceive septime and attack the quarte line.

M.	P.
Engage in quarte.	Derobe.
Parry septime.	Derobe into quarte, and lunge.

The same from the sixte engagement.

Cut over and disengage, to deceive sixte and attack the quarte line.

M.	P.
Engage in quarte (with point high).	Cut over.
Parry sixte.	Disengage into quarte, and lunge.

The same from the sixte engagement.

Cut over and derobe, to deceive sixte and attack the octave line.

M.	P.
Engage in quarte (point raised).	Cut over.
Parry sixte.	Derobe into octave, and lunge.

The same from the sixte engagement.

FROM THE ENGAGEMENTS IN THE LOW LINES.

Over and under, to deceive quarte and attack the septime line.

M.	P.
Engage in septime.	Derobe.
Parry quarte.	Derobe into septime, and lunge.

The same from the octave engagement.

One, two, to deceive octave and attack the septime line.

M.	P.
Engage in septime.	Disengage.
Parry octave.	Disengage into septime, and lunge.

The same from the octave engagement.

Disengage and derobe, to deceive octave and attack the sixte line.

M.	P.
Engage in septime.	Disengage.
Parry octave.	Derobe into sixte, and lunge.

COMBINED SIMPLE PARRIES.

The master must now, by means of the following lessons, make perfectly clear to the pupil the various ways there are of defeating the foregoing attacks by means of combinations of simple parries; he must impress on him the necessity of always engaging with opposition, or covering the line on which the engagement is formed, so as to make the straight thrust an impossibility, either as a direct attack or as a feint; and he should explain that those lessons, in which the master adopts the medium guard, are only given in order to teach the pupil how to take advantage of the mistake when made by an opponent in loose play.

The master should now close to half distance.

One, two, defeated by sixte and quarte.

Engage in quarte.

M.	P.
Disengage.	Parry sixte.
Disengage.	Parry quarte, and riposte.

Change to sixte.
Disengage.   Parry quarte.
Disengage.   Parry sixte, and riposte.

One, two, defeated by sixte and octave.

Engage in quarte.

M.	P.
Disengage.	Parry sixte.
Disengage (or derobe).	Parry octave, and riposte.
Change to sixte.	
Disengage.	Parry quarte.
Disengage (or derobe).	Parry septime, and riposte.

Under and over, defeated by septime and quarte.

Engage in quarte.

M.	P.
Derobe.	Parry septime.
Derobe.	Parry quarte, and riposte.
Change to sixte.	
Derobe.	Parry octave.
Derobe.	Parry sixte, and riposte.

Cut over and disengage, defeated by sixte and quarte.

Engage in quarte.

M.	P.
Cut over.	Parry sixte.
Disengage.	Parry quarte, and riposte.
Change to sixte.	
Cut over.	Parry quarte.
Disengage.	Parry sixte, and riposte.

Cut over and disengage, defeated by sixte and octave.

Engage in quarte.

M.	P.
Cut over.	Parry sixte.
Disengage (or derobe).	Parry octave, and riposte.
Change to sixte.	
Cut over.	Parry quarte.
Disengage (or derobe).	Parry septime, and riposte.

From the Engagements in the Low Lines.

Over and under, defeated by quarte and septime.

Engage in septime.

M.	P.
Derobe.	Parry quarte.
Derobe	Parry septime, and riposte.
Change to octave.	
Derobe.	Parry sixte.
Derobe.	Parry octave, and riposte.

One, two, defeated by octave and septime.

Engage in septime.

M.	P.
Disengage.	Parry octave.
Disengage.	Parry septime, and riposte.
Change to octave.	
Disengage.	Parry septime.
Disengage.	Parry octave, and riposte.

One, two, defeated by octave and sixte.

Engage in septime.

M.	P.
Disengage.	Parry octave.
Disengage (or derobe).	Parry sixte, and riposte.
Change to octave.	
Disengage.	Parry septime.
Disengage (or derobe).	Parry quarte, and riposte.

THE HALF-COUNTER.

The half-counter is a defensive movement which carries the enemy's point from a low line to the high line on the opposite side, or from a high line to the opposite low line. The former is the most to be recommended, as being the safest.

The action of the half-counter is precisely the opposite of " keeping captive." In the latter case we compel the opponent to remain on one side of our blade, while in the former we equally compel him to cross to the opposite line. The half-counter, therefore, is extremely useful as a variety of defence ; it is performed as follows :—

Engage in quarte.

M.	P.
Derob .	Parry septime.
Derobe.	Parry sixte and riposte.
Change to sixte.	
Derobe.	Parry octave.
Derobe.	Parry quarte and riposte.

THE BLINDFOLD LESSONS.—II.

SIMPLE PARRIES DECEIVED, AND THE BLADE FOUND AGAIN BY A SIMPLE PARRY.

1. Engage in quarte. Cover. Shut your eyes. I disengage, you parry sixte, I disengage again, you parry quarte and riposte. On guard.

2. Engage in sixte. Cover, etc. I disengage, you parry quarte, I disengage again, you parry sixte and riposte. On guard. You have thus parried my attack of "one, two."

3. Engage in quarte. Cover. Shut your eyes. I disengage, you parry sixte, I disengage again (or derobe), you parry octave and riposte. On guard.

4. Engage in sixte. Cover, etc. I disengage, you parry quarte, I disengage again (or derobe), you parry septime and riposte. On guard. You have again defeated my "one, two," but by a different movement.

5. Engage in quarte. Cover. Shut your eyes. I derobe (or disengage), you parry septime, I derobe again, you parry quarte and riposte. On guard.

6. Engage in sixte. Cover, etc. I derobe (or disengage), you parry octave, I derobe again, you parry sixte and riposte. On guard. You have here defeated my "under and over," keeping me "captive" on the line in which we were engaged.

7. Engage in quarte. Cover. Shut your eyes. I derobe, you parry septime, I derobe again, you raise your point and carry me over to the sixte line and riposte. On guard.

8. Engage in sixte. Cover, etc. I derobe, you parry octave, I derobe again, you raise your point and carry me over to the quarte line and riposte. On guard. You have again defeated my "under and over," but this time with the "half-counter."

ATTACKS CONSISTING OF THREE MOVEMENTS TO DECEIVE TWO SIMPLE PARRIES.

Thrust and one, two, to deceive quarte and sixte.

M.	P.
Engage in quarte medium.	Straight arm.
Parry quarte.	Disengage.
Parry sixte.	Disengage and lunge.
Change to sixte.	
Engage in sixte medium.	Straight arm.
Parry sixte.	Disengage.
Parry quarte.	Disengage and lunge.

Thrust and under and over, to deceive quarte and septime.

M.	P.
Engage in quarte medium.	Straight arm.
Parry quarte.	Derobe.
Parry septime.	Derobe and lunge.
Change to sixte.	
Engage in sixte medium.	Straight arm.
Parry sixte.	Derobe.
Parry octave.	Derobe and lunge.

One, two, three, to deceive sixte and quarte.

M.	P.
Engage in quarte.	Disengage.
Parry sixte.	Disengage.
Parry quarte.	Disengage and lunge.

Execute the same from the sixte engagement.

Under, over and under, to deceive septime and quarte.

M.	P.
Engage in quarte.	Derobe.
Parry septime.	Derobe.
Parry quarte.	Derobe and lunge.

Execute the same from the sixte engagement.

Disengage and under and over, to deceive sixte and octave.

M.	P.
Engage in quarte.	Disengage.
Parry sixte.	Derobe.
Parry octave.	Derobe and lunge.

Execute the same from the sixte engagement.

Cut over and one, two, to deceive sixte and quarte.

M.	P.
Engage in quarte.	Cut over.
Parry sixte.	Disengage.
Parry quarte.	Disengage and lunge.

Execute the same from sixte.

ATTACKS IN THREE MOVEMENTS DEFEATED BY COMBINED SIMPLE PARRIES.

The master should close to half distance.

One, two, three, defeated by sixte, quarte, and sixte.

M.	P.
Disengage.	Parry sixte.
Disengage.	Parry quarte.
Disengage.	Parry sixte and riposte.

The same from sixte, defeating by quarte, sixte, and quarte.

One, two three, defeated by sixte, quarte, and septime.

M.	P.
Disengage.	Parry sixte.
Disengage.	Parry quarte.
Disengage (or derobe).	Parry septime and riposte.

The same from sixte, defeating by quarte, sixte, and octave.

Under, over, and under, defeated by septime, quarte, and septime.

M.	P.
Derobe.	Parry septime.
Derobe.	Parry quarte.
Derobe.	Parry septime and riposte.

The same from sixte, defeating by octave, sixte, and octave.

Disengage and under and over, defeated by sixte, octave, and sixte.

M.	P.
Disengage.	Parry sixte.
Derobe.	Parry octave.
Derobe.	Parry sixte and riposte.

The same from sixte, defeating by quarte, septime, and quarte.

Disengage and under and over, defeated by sixte, octave, and half-counter.

M.	P.
Disengage.	Parry sixte.
Derobe.	Parry octave.
Derobe.	Parry quarte and riposte.

The same from sixte, defeating with quarte, septime, and sixte.

Cut over and one, two, defeated by sixte, quarte, and sixte.

M.	P.
Cut over.	Parry sixte.
Disengage.	Parry quarte.
Disengage.	Parry sixte and riposte.

The same from sixte, defeated by quarte, sixte, and quarte.

Cut over and one, two, defeated by sixte, quarte, and septime.

M.	P.
Cut over.	Parry sixte.
Disengage.	Parry quarte.
Disengage (or derobe).	Parry septime and riposte.

The same from sixte, defeating with quarte, sixte, and octave.

/THE BLINDFOLD LESSONS.—III.

Two Simple Parries Deceived, and the Blade Found by a Simple Parry.

1. Engage in quarte. Cover. Shut your eyes. I disengage, you parry sixte, I disengage again, you parry quarte, I disengage a third time, and you parry sixte and riposte. On guard.

2. Engage in sixte. Cover, etc. I disengage, you parry quarte, I disengage again, you parry sixte, I disengage a third time, and you parry quarte and riposte. On guard. You have here defeated my " one, two, three."

3. Engage in quarte. Cover. Shut your eyes. I disengage, you parry sixte, I disengage again, you parry quarte, I disengage a third time, and you parry septime and riposte. On guard.

4. Engage in sixte. Cover, etc. I disengage, you parry quarte, I disengage again, you parry sixte, I disengage again, and you parry octave and riposte. On guard. You have again defeated my " one, two, three," but you have varied your defence by stopping my third movement with a parry in the low line.

5. Engage in quarte. Cover. Shut your eyes. I derobe, you parry septime, I derobe again, you parry quarte, I derobe a third time, and you parry septime and riposte. On guard.

6. Engage in sixte. Cover, etc. I derobe, you parry octave, I derobe again, you parry sixte, I derobe a third time, and you parry octave and riposte. On guard. You have here defeated my " under, over, and under."

7. Engage in quarte. Cover. Shut your eyes. I disengage, you parry sixte, I derobe, you parry octave, I derobe again, and you parry sixte and riposte. On guard.

8. Engage in sixte. Cover, etc. I disengage, you parry quarte, I derobe, you parry septime, I derobe again, and you parry quarte and riposte. On guard. You have thus defeated my " disengage and under and over."

9. Engage in quarte. Cover. Shut your eyes. I disengage, you parry sixte, I derobe, you parry octave, I derobe again, and you carry me over to quarte and riposte. On guard.

10. Engage in sixte. Cover, etc. I disengage, you parry quarte, I derobe, you parry septime, I derobe again, and you carry me over to sixte and riposte. On guard. You have again defeated my " disengage and under and over," but this time with the assistance of the half-counter.

THE COUNTERS, OR CIRCULAR PARRIES.

Up to the present we have only studied the simple parries ; we now come to another series—the counters.

The counter is effected from any one of the our positions of quarte, sixte, septime, and octave, and also, of course, from those with the hand in pronation, by following with a circular movement the attacking blade during its disengagement, and so bringing it back to the original line from which it started. The counters which I shall employ are as follows :—

Engage in quarte.

Counter-quarte.—On my disengagement pass you point under my blade and bring it round again to the quarte line, taking care that on the completion of your parry your point shall again be in line with my face.

Engage in sixte.

Counter-sixte.—On my disengagement pass your point underneath my blade and bring me back to the sixte line.

Engage in septime.

Counter-septime.—On my disengagement pass your point over my blade and bring me back to septime.

Engage in octave.

Counter-octave.—On my disengagement pass your point over my blade and bring me back to octave.

As soon as the pupil understands these counter-parries he must be taught to combine with them the riposte.

It will now be seen that we have three varieties of parry with which we can defeat an attack commenced by a simple disengagement. We are, for the sake of example, engaged in quarte ; and we defeat the attack (1) by passing our blade over to sixte, and so parrying the thrust in the line against which it is directed ; (2) by arresting the movement half-way with the parry of septime ; and (3) by following the attacking blade round as it disengages, and bringing it back to the original line by the parry of counter-quarte. It is clear, therefore, that after the first disengagement the game is under the control of the defender, as in order to effect a hit the assailant has to deceive whichever of the three parries the other chooses to adopt.

THE BLINDFOLD LESSONS.—IV.

ON THE COUNTER-PARRIES.

Engage in quarte. Cover. Shut your eyes.
I disengage, parry counter-quarte and riposte. On guard.

Engage in sixte. Cover. Shut your eyes.
I disengage, parry counter-sixte and riposte. On guard.

Engage in septime.   Cover.   Shut your eyes.
I disengage, parry counter-septime and riposte.   On guard.

Engage in octave.
I disengage, parry counter-octave and riposte.   On guard.

COUNTER-PARRIES DECEIVED.

Our next study must be the attack made by deceiving the counter, by the movement which is technically known as the " double."

M.	P.
1. Engage in quarte.	Disengage.
Parry counter-quarte.	Disengage and lunge.
2. Engage in sixte.	Disengage.
Parry counter-sixte.	Disengage and lunge.
3. Engage in quarte.	Disengage.
Parry counter-quarte.	Derobe and lunge.
4. Engage in sixte.	Disengage.
Parry counter-sixte.	Derobe and lunge.
5. Engage in septime.	Disengage.
Parry counter-septime.	Disengage and lunge.
6. Engage in octave.	Disengage.
Parry counter-octave.	Disengage and lunge.
7. Engage in septime.	Disengage.
Parry counter-septime.	Derobe and lunge.
8. Engage in octave.	Disengage.
Parry counter-octave.	Derobe and lunge.

The Double Defeated.

The master will take his place at half distance.

Engage in quarte.

M.	P.
1. Disengage.	Parry counter-quarte.
Disengage.	Parry sixte and riposte.
	On guard.
2. Disengage.	Parry counter-quarte.
Disengage (or derobe).	Parry septime and riposte.
	On guard.
3. Disengage.	Parry counter-quarte.
Disengage.	Parry counter-quarte and riposte.
	On guard.

Engage in sixte.

M.	P.
1. Disengage.	Parry counter-sixte.
Disengage.	Parry quarte and riposte.
	On guard.
2. Disengage.	Parry counter-sixte.
Disengage (or derobe).	Parry octave and riposte.
	On guard.
3. Disengage.	Parry counter-sixte.
Disengage.	Parry counter-sixte and riposte.
	On guard.

We have thus defeated the " double " in the upper lines

by three varieties of parry, but in the low lines I do not think the " twice counter " advisable.

Engage in septime.

M.	P.
1. Disengage.	Parry counter-septime.
Disengage.	Parry octave and riposte.
On guard.	

2. Disengage.	Parry counter-septime.
Disengage (or derobe).	Parry quarte and riposte.
On guard.	

3. Disengage.	Parry counter-septime.
Derobe.	Parry sixte and riposte.
On guard.	

Engage in octave.

M.	P.
1. Disengage.	Parry counter-octave.
Disengage.	Parry septime and riposte.
On guard.	

2. Disengage.	Parry counter-octave.
Disengage (or derobe).	Parry sixte and riposte.
On guard.	

| 3. Disengage. | Parry counter-octave. |
| Derobe. | Parry quarte and riposte. |

The " one, two " defeated by a simple and a counter.

Engage in quarte.

M.	P.
Disengage.	Parry sixte.
Disengage.	Parry counter-sixte and ri- poste.

On guard.

Engage in sixte.	
Disengage.	Parry quarte.
Disengage.	Parry counter-quarte and riposte.

On guard.

The "one, two, three" defeated by two simples and a counter.

Engage in quarte.

M.	P.
Disengage.	Parry sixte.
Disengage.	Parry quarte.
Disengage.	Parry counter-quarte and riposte.

On guard.

Engage in sixte.	
Disengage.	Parry quarte.
Disengage.	Parry sixte.
Disengage.	Parry counter-sixte and ri- poste.

On guard.

The half-counter deceived.

M.	P.
Engage in quarte.	Derobe.
Parry septime.	Derobe.
Parry sixte.	Disengage and lunge.

On guard.

The above defeated.

Derobe.	Parry septime.
Derobe.	Parry sixte.
Disengage.	Parry counter-sixte and ri-
	poste.

On guard.

From the sixte engagement.

M.	P.
Engage in sixte.	Derobe.
Parry octave.	Derobe.
Parry quarte.	Disengage and lunge.

On guard.

The above defeated.

Derobe.	Parry octave.
Derobe.	Parry quarte.
Disengage.	Parry counter-quarte and
	riposte.

On guard.

FURTHER ATTACKS AGAINST COMBINED COUNTER AND SIMPLE PARRIES.

One, two, and deceive the counter.

M.	P.
Engage in quarte.	Disengage.
Parry sixte.	Disengage.
Parry counter-sixte.	Disengage and lunge.

On guard.

The above defeated.

Disengage.	Parry sixte.
Disengage.	Parry counter-sixte.
Disengage.	Parry quarte or octave and riposte.

On guard.

From the sixte engagement.

Engage in sixte.	Disengage.
Parry quarte.	Disengage.
Parry counter-quarte.	Disengage and lunge.

On guard.

The above deceived.

Disengage.	Parry quarte.
Disengage.	Parry counter-quarte.
Disengage.	Parry sixte or septime and riposte.

On guard.

Double and disengage, to deceive counter-quarte and sixte.

M.	P.
Engage in quarte.	Disengage.
Parry counter-quarte.	Disengage.
Parry sixte.	Disengage and lunge.

On guard.

The above defeated.

Disengage.	Parry counter-quarte.
Disengage.	Parry sixte.
Disengage.	Parry counter-sixte and riposte.

On guard.

Engage in sixte.	Disengage.
Parry counter-sixte.	Disengage.
Parry quarte.	Disengage and lunge.

On guard.

The above defeated.	
Disengage.	Parry counter-sixte.
Disengage.	Parry quarte.
Disengage.	Parry counter-quarte and riposte.

On guard.

Counter-quarte and septime deceived by the derobement.

M.	P.
Engage in quarte.	Disengage.
Parry counter-quarte.	Derobe.
Parry septime.	Derobe or disengage and lunge.

On guard.

The above defeated by a counter and two simples.	
Disengage.	Parry counter-quarte.
Disengage.	Parry septime.
Derobe (or disengage).	Parry quarte and riposte.

On guard.

Engage in sixte.	Disengage.
Parry counter-sixte.	Derobe.
Parry octave.	Derobe or disengage and lunge.

The above defeated.	
Disengage.	Parry counter-sixte.
Derobe.	Parry octave.
Derobe (or disengage).	Parry sixte and riposte.

When the derobement is used, the defender may vary the play by employing the half-counter.

4

THE BLINDFOLD LESSONS.—V.

ON COUNTERS AND SIMPLES COMBINED.

1. Engage in quarte. Cover. Shut your eyes. I disengage, parry sixte, I disengage again, parry counter-sixte and riposte. On guard.

2. Engage in sixte. Cover, etc. I disengage, parry quarte, I disengage again, parry counter-quarte. On guard. You have defeated my "one, two" from both engagements.

3. Engage in quarte. Cover. Shut your eyes. I disengage, parry counter-quarte, I deceive it, parry sixte and riposte. On guard.

4. Engage in sixte. Cover, etc. I disengage, parry counter-sixte, I deceive it, parry quarte and riposte. On guard.

5. Engage in quarte. Cover, etc. I disengage, parry counter-quarte, I deceive it, parry septime and riposte. On guard.

6. Engage in sixte. Cover, etc. I disengage, parry counter-sixte, I deceive it, parry octave and riposte. On guard. You have thus defeated my "double" in two ways from both engagements.

7. Engage in quarte. Cover. Shut your eyes. I disengage, parry counter-quarte, I deceive it, parry sixte, I deceive that, parry counter-sixte and riposte. On guard.

8. Engage in sixte. Cover, etc. I disengage, parry counter-sixte, I deceive it, parry quarte, I deceive again, parry counter-quarte and riposte. On guard.

9. Engage in quarte. Cover. Shut your eyes. I disengage, parry counter-quarte, I derobe, parry septime, I derobe again, parry quarte and riposte. On guard.

10. Engage in quarte. Cover, etc. I disengage, parry

counter-quarte, I deceive it, parry septime, I disengage again, parry counter-septime and riposte. On guard.

11. Engage in quarte. Cover, etc. I disengage, parry sixte, I disengage, parry quarte, I disengage again, parry counter-quarte and riposte. On guard.

12. Engage in quarte. Cover, etc. I derobe, parry septime, I derobe again, parry sixte, I disengage, parry counter-sixte and riposte. On guard.

From the sixte engagement.

13. Engage in sixte. Cover, etc. I disengage, parry counter-sixte, I deceive it, parry octave, I deceive again, parry sixte and riposte. On guard.

14. Engage in sixte. Cover, etc. I disengage, parry counter-sixte, I deceive it, parry octave, I disengage, parry counter-octave and riposte. On guard.

15. Engage in sixte. Cover, etc. I disengage, parry quarte, I deceive it, parry sixte, I deceive again, parry counter-sixte and riposte. On guard.

16. Engage in sixte. Cover, etc. I derobe, parry octave, I derobe again, parry quarte, I disengage, parry counter quarte, and riposte. On guard.

An intelligent master will be able to form on the foregoing blindfold lessons any further variations which the case of his pupil may need—as, for instance, the combination which we may describe as the *grand tour* of the target, in which each line is defended in its turn by a simple and a counter-parry without any break in the movement, as follows : Engage in quarte. Cover, etc. I disengage, parry counter-quarte, I derobe, parry septime, I disengage, parry counter-septime, I disengage again, parry octave, again I disengage, parry counter-octave, I derobe, parry sixte, I disengage, parry counter-sixte, I disengage again, parry quarte and riposte. On guard.

THE COMPOUND RIPOSTE.

This is a riposte accompanied by a disengagement or some such other movement; it becomes necessary when the opportunity for the instantaneous direct riposte has been lost through delay, and therefore is applicable at the moment when the opponent attempts to recover; it should never be attempted while he is still on the lunge, lest he should remise, and so cause an exchanged hit which would be disastrous to both. It should consist of not more than two movements, one the feint and the other the true attack, because there will not be time for more; nor is the opponent likely to follow our blade in such a manner as to make more possible.

The compound riposte in one movement is useful when the opponent's sword-hand is so placed as to impede the direct riposte. It is very often necessary to support it with the lunge.

The compound ripostes are as follow :—

Having parried quarte or counter-quarte, derobe, and thrust in septime. Disengage and thrust in sixte. Cut over and thrust in sixte. Feint a straight thrust and derobe. Feint a straight thrust and disengage. "One, two" or "double" according to the parry used by the opponent. Under and over. Having parried sixte or counter-sixte, derobe and thrust in octave. Disengage and thrust in quarte. Cut over and thrust in quarte. Feint a straight thrust and derobe. Feint a straight thrust and disengage. "One, two" or "double." Under and over. Having parried septime, derobe. Over and under. Feint straight thrust and disengage. Having parried octave, derobe. Over and under. Thrust and disengage.

Movements of Force or Attacks on the Blade.

The object of these attacks is to drive the opponent's point out of line when it has assumed a too menacing position, and they are also employed as feints in conjunction with other movements. There are various ways of attacking the blade—namely, the change, the double engagement, the pressure, the coulé, the froissé, the beat, the double beat, the beat in the opposite line, and the bind.

The Change.

This, as also the double engagement, is extremely useful to cover an advance rendered necessary by the opponent being a little out of measure.

Being engaged in quarte.

Pass your point underneath the opponent's blade, and engage it again in the sixte line, when, if he does not answer by covering himself, lunge at once ; if he covers, disengage or derobe and lunge ; these may be followed by any compound movements which the form of his parry may render necessary.

The Double Engagement.

From quarte.

Pass your point underneath the opponent's blade and engage him lightly in sixte, and as he moves to cover change again to the quarte line, and attack as directed in the " change."

The Pressure.

With the *action of the fingers only* apply a light, quick, lateral pressure to the opposing blade, and, if it yields, lunge.

The "Coulé."

This is essentially useful when the opponent's covering is either imperfect or weak.

Advance the point until the arm is perfectly straight, causing your blade to *glide very lightly* down the whole length of the opponent's blade, and lunge.

The coulé is extremely useful when used as a feint in combination with other movements.

The "Froissé."

Without in the least withdrawing your blade from that of the opponent, press sharply and suddenly upon it both with a lateral and a downward movement, and, as his blade yields, lunge.

The Beat.

Withdraw your blade slightly from that of the opponent, and immediately return to it with a sharp, dry, lateral rap, and, as it is forced aside, lunge.

The False Beat.

This term is applied to the foregoing movement when it is employed as a feint.

The Double Beat.

This can only be executed from the sixte engagement.

Pass your point under the opposing blade, and, as you arrive in the quarte line, deliver a light upward beat close to its point, then instantly cut over and deliver a very strong downward beat with a "froissé" movement in sixte straightening the arm at the same time and lunging instantly.

The Beat in the Opposite Line.

This is simply a beat preceded by a disengagement, and the command used by the best French masters is—being engaged in quarte—" beat in sixte," on which you disengage and beat in one movement, and, as his blade yields, lunge.

Binding.

Binding is the action of forcing the opposing blade from its position in a high line to the low line on the opposite side, or *vice versâ*, such as from quarte to octave or from septime to sixte; it should only be attempted when the adversary's arm is a good deal extended and his point nearly level.

From quarte press slightly on his blade, and at the same time drop your point downwards on the outside of it, circling round it without quitting contact, the forte of your foil acting on the foible of his, and so bring it round to the position of octave. This, when forcibly executed with the hand in pronation, will disarm the opponent.

The Attacks of Force Employed as Feints.

The most useful of these are the pressure, the coulé, and the false beat, and occasionally the bind.

Engage in quarte.

Press, coulé, false beat, and disengage or derobe, following with compound movement according to the parries affected by the opponent.

Combinations of Attack, Riposte, and Counter-Riposte.

These combinations form a connecting link between the various foregoing lessons and the assault or " loose play."

I here record only a small number of them, but any teacher of ordinary intelligence should be able to arrange others according to the requirements of each individual pupil.

When the counter-riposte is made by the pupil, the master should allow himself to be touched.

M.	P.
1. Engage in quarte.	Disengage and lunge.
Parry counter-quarte and lunge.	Parry quarte, derobe and lunge.
(Parry septime.)	

On guard.

Reverse the practice.

2. Engage in quarte.	Derobe and lunge.
Parry septime, disengage and lunge.	Parry counter-septime, derobe and lunge.
(Parry quarte.) ·	

On guard.

Reverse the practice.

3. Engage in sixte.	Disengage and lunge.
Parry counter-sixte and lunge.	Parry sixte, disengage and lunge.
(Parry quarte.)	

On guard.

Reverse the practice.

4. Engage in sixte.	Disengage and lunge.
Parry counter-sixte, derobe and lunge.	Parry septime (*i.e.*, half-counter) and lunge.
(Parry septime, or quarte.)	

ABSENCE.

Absence is the temporary withdrawal from contact with the opposing blade, either for the purpose of preventing the enemy from divining our intention by the sense of touch, or by showing a great opening to induce him to risk an attack.

TIME ATTACKS.

The time attack is that made at the moment when the adversary is meditating or preparing his attack; it is always a direct attack, and must be made with strong opposition.

THE STOP-THRUST.

This movement has much the same effect as the time, and is essentially useful against one who rushes violently on his antagonist. As far as its form is concerned, I prefer the Italian style, in which the left foot is slipped back, and the right arm extended until the position of lunge is attained. It is further developed in the form of the " under stop-thrust," by dropping the body forward, and placing the palm of the left hand on the ground about in line with the right foot (*vide* " Cold Steel ").

THE REMISE.

The remise is a second hit, the first having been parried, made without recovering from the lunge, and without attempting to find the adverse blade. It is under most circumstances considered extremely bad fencing, owing to the great risk of being touched at the same moment by the riposte. *But* when the opponent, in parrying the first thrust, carries his point so much off the line as to make the instantaneous riposte impossible, the remise becomes not only a permissible but also a highly artistic stroke.

The Reprise.

The reprise is a second hit given when on the lunge, but after having previously found the opponent's blade, so as to prevent his riposting.

The Redouble.

The redouble is a new attack made without the slightest pause after having recovered to " guard."

Exchanged Hits.

When both combatants touch at the same time the hits are thus termed. For further information about them and their validity refer to the Rules.

Drawing Back the Hand.

The action of drawing back the sword, as a sort of commencement of the attack, and delivering a stabbing stroke like that of a poniard, is a vicious habit to which some people are much addicted, and one which any student of fence, who desires to achieve a reputation as a swordsman, must scrupulously avoid ; it is fearfully dangerous, owing to the strong possibility of breaking the blade and the utter impossibility of checking the thrust, and so inflicting a perhaps mortal wound on the opponent ; it is in reality the last resource of a hopelessly bad swordsman to score a hit which he is unable to effect by more legitimate means. There is but one sensible way of treating a man who persists in using this style of attack, and that is to refuse flatly to fence with him at all.

CAVÉ.

The " cavé " is the exact reverse to " opposition." It consists of attacking usually the inner line with the hand in pronation and carried towards the outside—that is to say, away from the opponent's sword, the arm and the blade forming an angle. Some men attempt it in the hope of getting round the parry, and so reaching their opponent ; but in doing so they shorten their reach, and so are obliged to advance, which renders them liable to a time attack. When the cavé is used against the outer lines, the hand is in supination.

TO GAIN GROUND ON THE LUNGE.

This movement may be used against an opponent who is given to retiring precipitately when attacked. When on the lunge, instead of recovering to guard in the usual way, bring up the left foot until the correct distance between the feet has been attained, and so take possession of the ground which he has lost.

SLIPPING.

This movement is more applicable to the sabre than to the foil. It is used when the attack is made upon an advanced part, such as the arm or leg, by withdrawing the part and delivering a thrust or cut at the same time. In slipping the leg the haunches must be well drawn back, so as to get them as much out of the way as possible (*vide* Frontispiece).

TRAVERSING.

This movement is useful at times in an open space. It consists of shifting ground to either flank, in order to force the enemy into a disadvantageous position, or to extricate oneself from something similar.

Traversing to the left is effected by moving the left foot off the line about six inches, and then bringing the right foot in front of it again in the new line.

In traversing to the right, the right foot moves first, and care must always be taken not to cross the feet.

THE SALUTE.

When about to fence before an audience it is customary for the two combatants to offer their public this courteous recognition before commencing their assault, and it is best done as follows :—

From the first position.

Salute to the left.—(1) Bend the sword-arm, bringing the elbow close to the body, with the hand on a level with the chin, and the palm turned towards the face. (2) Lower the foil to the left, the arm half extended, the hand in supination, the blade horizontal, and the head turned to the left.

Salute to the right, in a similar manner, but with the hand in pronation.

Salute to the front, as usual.

On guard.

This is all that is *absolutely necessary* in a public performance. Many masters teach, and most modern books contain, a much more elaborate salute, known in French as *le mur.* It is an elegant show exercise ; but I never could think it of any real practical value, and I do not recommend a student of fence to trouble about it until he has made himself thoroughly efficient in the use of his weapon as a fighting arm.

THE ASSAULT.

The assault, or "loose play," is the exact imitation of a combat with real swords, in which the opponents bring into use, as occasion may demand, all the manœuvres which the master has imparted to them in the lessons on the plastron, and in it no movement ought to be attempted which would be attended with too much risk were the point sharp.

The student of fence must never imagine that because his master permits him to make the assault, that frees him from the necessity of taking lessons. A lesson should be taken every day on which he attends the fencing-room ; it is *absolutely* necessary, not only in order to ensure further progress, but also to avoid the danger of lapsing into bad habits, which the neglect of it is certain to cause, and soon degenerating into that extremely unpleasant class of person who openly announces that he only frequents the fencing-room for the purpose of "getting a sweat," and, having made this announcement, immediately proceeds to inflict himself on the best swordsman he can find in the room.

The beginner should not be allowed to make his first assaults with one of his own calibre, as, being both of them inexperienced, they are certain to make more or less awkward movements, and so put each other more and more wrong ; but he should fence at first only with his master, who, on his part, should accommodate his play to that of his pupil, and should carefully explain the cause of any failure in the latter's parries and attacks.

A combatant when touched should invariably acknowledge the hit in a tone loud enough to be heard not only by the opponent, but also by the bystanders.

PART II.—THE SINGLESTICK AND SABRE.

PART II.

THE SINGLESTICK AND SABRE.

———◆———

THE system of play with these two weapons is one and the same; the singlestick being nothing more than a cheap (and nasty) substitute for the fencing sabre as used in every country except our own; they are employed both for cutting and thrusting.

The sabre should be a *light* one, thickened almost into a button at the point, and supple enough to obviate any risk of inflicting injury in delivering the thrust. The best pattern that I am acquainted with is that made by Messrs. Pillin, of Gerrard Street, Soho, according to my directions, as it combines all the above qualities, and has, moreover, a grip sufficiently long to enable it to sit comfortably in the hand with the thumb in its proper place, while its shell is very broad, and affords ample protection to both hand and forearm.

When the light sabre is used, the helmet should be constructed with close wire-work, like that of the mask, as a guarantee against the penetration of the point.

THE PARTS OF THE SABRE.

The sabre, like the foil, has its two great component parts,—the hilt and the blade; and this latter has, in addition to the "forte" and the "foible," its defensive and offensive portions, the "false edge," that sharp part of the back which extends from the point to the place where the grooving usually begins, a distance of about eight inches.

How to Hold the Sabre or Stick.

The fingers must be lightly but firmly closed round the grip, with the thumb extended along the back of it, the centre knuckles being in line with the edge; the thumb may, however, during an encounter, sometimes be shifted and placed round the grip similarly to the fingers (Fig. 18).

First Position.

The first position is similar to that used in the foil lessons, save that the left hand is closed and placed on the hip, from which it is *not* removed during the execution of the lunge.

The Guards.

The Medium Guard.

The medium guard is the best suited for both attack and defence in this branch of our art. It is, like the medium of foil fencing, neither quarte nor tierce, but just between the two; the edge is inclined downwards, the point is opposite the opponent's face, the right hand and

Fig. 18.

forearm entirely covered by the shell, and the elbow advanced some four inches in front of the body (Fig. 19).

The position is known as quarte medium or tierce medium, according to the side on which the blades are engaged. This guard is the more to be recommended owing to the absence of any strain on the arm or shoulder, which is often the effect of other positions.

Fig. 19.

The Resting Medium.

The sword-hand is now lowered until the pummel rests on the thigh some six or eight inches above the knee. The arm now is in a state of absolute repose, which will be found useful in a long encounter at times when the opponent happens to be out of reach.

The Hanging Guard.

This old-fashioned position has its use as a shelter under which to recover after having made an attack, whether successful or otherwise ; it is a safeguard against an honest riposte, and also against a foul blow, which some ill-conditioned fellows are wont to give, instead of acknowledging when they are touched ; it is formed by dropping the point, turning the edge up, raising the hand a little higher than the head, and looking at the opponent under the forte of the sword (Fig. 21).

PREPARATORY LESSONS.

THE MOULINETS.

The object of these exercises is to impart strength and flexibility to the wrist joint, from which all the cuts should in the main proceed.

They consist of six cuts,—the 1st, a diagonal cut downwards from right to left ; the 2nd, a diagonal cut downwards from left to right ; the 3rd, diagonal upwards from right to left ; the 4th, diagonal upwards from left to right ; the 5th, horizontal from right to left ; and the 6th, horizontal from left to right.

To assist the beginner a circular target a few inches in diameter, with two diagonal lines and one horizontal line passing through its centre drawn upon it, should be hung on the wall at about the height of a man's shoulder ; the lines indicate the course taken by the six cuts.

The moulinets must be executed with the wrist and fingers only, and never with the elbow or shoulder ; they must be performed quite slowly at first in order to ensure correctness ; the speed must be gradually increased, and the circular movement repeated five or six times at least without stopping.

Moulinet 1.

Motion 1.—Extend the sword-arm completely, the hand to be in quarte, and the point a little raised, the hilt being at about the height of the chin, and the edge directed obliquely downwards towards the left.

Motion 2.—Drop the point diagonally downwards from right to left, taking care that the edge leads during the passage of the blade along the line of the target ; then allow the wrist to revolve, so as to bring the thumb downwards and the back of the hand and the flat of the blade opposite the left side, and cause the sword to describe a complete circle, thereby bringing it again to the position described in the first motion.

Moulinet 2.

Motion 1.—Extend the sword-arm, the hand to be in tierce, and the edge directed obliquely downwards towards the right.

Motion 2.—Drop the point diagonally downwards from left to right, and, after the sword has passed its line on the target, allow the wrist to revolve until its inside is uppermost and the point of the sword to the right rear ; complete the circle, and thus bring the sword again to No. 1.

Moulinet 3.

Motion 1.—Extend the sword-arm, the hilt being, as before, about the height of the chin, with the blade in the position of septime, the point being depressed about ten inches, and the edge directed obliquely upwards towards the left.

Motion 2.—Carry the edge diagonally upward from right to left, until it has passed the line on the target; then turn the back of the hand up, and complete the circle by dropping the point to the right rear, and thus bring the sword again to No. 1.

Moulinet 4.

Motion 1.—Extend the arm, the hilt being about the height of the chin, the blade assuming the position of seconde, the point depressed about ten inches, and the edge directed obliquely upwards towards the right.

Motion 2.—Carry the blade obliquely upwards from left to right until it has traversed the line on the target ; then allow the hand to revolve until the nails are uppermost, and thus continue the circle until the sword is again in the position of No. 1.

Moulinet 5.

Motion 1.—Extend the arm, the point of the sword to be directed about ten inches to the right of the target, with the edge towards the left.

Motion 2.—Carry the blade horizontally along the line of the target from right to left ; then turn the back of the hand up, and complete the circle by passing the point of the sword over the head in a position as nearly horizontal as possible, and thus come again to No. 1.

Moulinet 6.

Motion 1.—Extend the arm with the back of the hand up, edge to the right, and the point about ten inches to the left of the target.

Motion 2.—Carry the blade horizontally from left to right, and when it has passed the target turn the nails up and complete the circle above the head, returning to the position of No. 1 (Fig. 20).

The "figure of eight" consists of a continuous combination of moulinets 1 and 2, or 3 and 4.

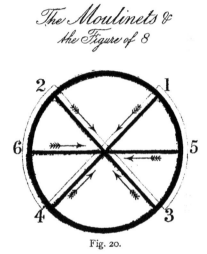

Fig. 20.

THE DIRECT ATTACKS.

The direct attack is that which is made upon any un covered part of the opponent's person without having had recourse to a previous movement for the purpose of creating such opening. It is of three kinds—namely, the cut with the true edge, the point, and the cut with the "false edge," to which latter I shall devote a special paragraph or two it is delivered either with or without a disengagement, which movement is made over the adversary's point in the case of a cut, as in the " cut over " of foil fencing, and under the blade when the thrust is used.

The cuts should be performed, not as a target, as in

Fig. 21.

the case of the moulinets, but in a personal lesson with the master ; and the student can practise them also, with advantage to himself, at home against a dummy.

Each cut is to be delivered on the full lunge (Fig. 21); and, whether it succeeds or whether it is parried, the swordsman must instantly recover to his guard. It must be given with that part of the blade in which lies the

"centre of percussion," about eight or ten inches from the
point; it must strike the object at the moment when
the foot reaches the ground on the lunge; and it must be
finished with a little jerk or spring of the wrist, followed by
a drawing movement.

To attempt to give two cuts (remise) on the same lunge
is bad swordsmanship, because a capable opponent is
certain to riposte immediately after parrying the first of
them (Fig. 21).

There are seven principal cuts, and they are directed at
specified parts of the body, as follows :—

Cut 1.—Deliver cut 1 of the moulinets at the opponent's
left cheek or neck.

Cut 2.—Deliver cut 2 of the moulinets at the right
cheek.

Cut 3.—Deliver cut 3 of the moulinets at the outside of
the right leg.

Cut 4.—Deliver cut 4 of the moulinets at the outside of
the right leg.

Cut 5.—Deliver cut 5 of the moulinets at the left side or
the belly.

Cut 6.—Deliver cut 6 of the moulinets at the right side
just under the ribs.

Cut 7.—Deliver a vertical downward cut at the centre of
the head.

As occasion may require these cuts may be directed at
parts other than those here named : for instance, cuts 1
and 2 may be given at the leg or at the sword-arm.

THE POINT.

If the point is given within the sword the hand must be
in supination, and if without in pronation.

The Parries.

These defensive movements are so closely allied to the parries employed in foil fencing that I shall adhere to the names used in that branch of the art.

Fig. 22.

The parries of primary importance are *quarte*, which, with its varieties of high and low, protects everything on the inside, from the top of the head to the base of the trunk, while *tierce* affords the corresponding cover to the outside ;

the outside of the leg is guarded by *seconde*, and the inside of it (should the opponent attempt so wicked a stroke) is guaranteed by *septime*.

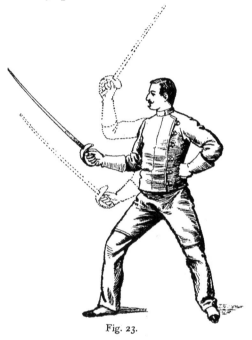

Fig. 23.

To Stop Cut 1.

Parry *quarte.*—Turn the hand to quarte, carrying it a little to the left, with the point slightly raised, and receive the cut on the full edge of the forte, as near the shell as possible (Fig. 22).

To Stop Cut 2.

Parry *tierce*.—Turn the nails down, carry the hand a little to the right, with the point slightly raised, and the edge directed towards the right front, and receive on the forte (Fig. 23).

To Stop Cut 3.

Parry *septime*.—Turn the edge to the left, carrying the hand a little to that side, drop the point in the form of septime, and receive on the forte (Fig 24).

To Stop Cut 4.

Parry *seconde*.—Turn the nails down, carry the hand a little to the right, drop the point to the position of seconde, and receive on the forte (Fig. 25).

To Stop Cut 5.

Parry *quarte* (low).—Turn the hand to quarte, drop it about as low as the thigh, and receive on the forte (Fig. 22).

To Stop Cut 6.

Parry *tierce* (low).—Turn the hand to tierce, dropping it to the level of the thigh, and receive on the forte (Fig. 23).

Fig. 24.

To Stop Cut 7.

Parry *quarte* (high).—Turn the hand to quarte, raise it about as high as the left temple, and receive on the forte at the angle where it meets the shell (Fig. 22).

Parry *tierce* (high).—Turn the hand to tierce, raise it to about the height of the right temple, and receive close to the shell (Fig. 23).

Auxiliary Parries.

The parries of high octave and high seconde, together with the primes high, central, and low, and the St. George (which is also a form of prime), should be regarded only as defences of an auxiliary nature, to be employed against a riposte or counter-riposte in the event of the hand being momentarily so placed as to render difficult a recovery to one of the first-named series. Of these the most important are the *high octave* and the *high prime*, as they defeat a riposte delivered over the blade after the parries of quarte or tierce; and against these powerful ripostes no other defence is possible.

Fig. 25.

Parry *high octave*.—Raise the hilt to a level with the top of the head, and, by relaxing the grip of the second, third, and fourth fingers, allow the blade to drop forward as nearly perpendicular as possible, with the edge to the right front, and receive cut 2 on the forte (Fig. 26).

Parry *high prime*.—Raise the hilt, turning the edge upwards, and bring it over to the left front, *taking care not to draw it in towards the body,* depress the point some six or eight inches, looking to the front *over* the right wrist, and receive cut 1 (Fig. 27).

Another high prime may, on emergency, be employed in the form of the " hanging guard," by raising the hilt a little

Fig. 26.

above the level of the top of the head, and looking at the opponent under the wrist.

The parry of *prime* defeats cut 5 by raising the hilt to the left front about as high as the shoulder, and dropping the point perpendicularly in the form of prime (Fig. 28).

By lowering the hand to about the level of the waist *low prime* is formed, which defends the inside of the leg (Fig. 28).

The St. George parries a vertical cut at the head, by raising the hand a little higher than the top of the head, the elbow to be well behind the hilt, the blade pointing to the left front, with the point a little depressed (Fig. 28).

Fig. 27.

The *high seconde* parries a cut at the right side, by raising the hand as high as the shoulder, lowering the point so that the blade is nearly perpendicular, and presenting the edge to the right front (Fig. 25).

THE FEINTS.

All feints with the sabre or stick should be made by

a crisp, quick little movement of the wrist and fingers only; and, as the opponent answers with his parry, the opening so gained must be attacked with precision and rapidity.

The student can assist both himself and his master very

Fig. 28.

considerably by practising the feints at a dummy of some kind when he is at home, taking care that the feint should be executed just before the foot rises from the second position (that of "guard"), and that the cut should be completed just as the foot touches the ground in the position of the lunge.

The following feints are, I think, the most effectual :—

Feint 1 at left cheek and cut 4 at leg.

,,	,,	,,	,,	2 at right cheek.
,,	2 at right cheek		,,	1 at left cheek.
,,	,,	,,	,,	5 at left side.
,,	,,	,,	,,	3 at leg.
,,	,,	,,	,,	4 at leg.
,,	4 at leg		,,	2 at right cheek.
,,	,,		,,	1 at left cheek.
,,	5 at left side		,,	2 at right cheek.
,,	point in sixte at face		,,	6 at right side.
,,	,,	,,	,,	4 at leg.

ADVANCED LESSONS.

ON THE PARRY AND RIPOSTE.

The object of the feint is to affect the nerve of the opponent through the medium of his eye, and therefore it is necessary so to train the pupil that he may gradually acquire the habit of not being influenced by it ; I therefore, in the ensuing lessons of attacks and parries with their various ripostes, prescribe a feint (any that may be applicable to the case), which is to precede the initial attack, and of this feint the pupil must be instructed to take not the slightest notice, *but to parry only the real attack.*

When the pupil delivers the riposte the master must allow himself to be touched, and to this end he should arm himself with sufficient padded armour to protect himself from injury ; but when he himself delivers it he must cause the pupil to execute the proper parry.

6

Ripostes from the Quarte Parries.

M.	P.
Feint 2 and cut 1.	Parry quarte, cut 2 over the blade.
(Parry high octave.)	
	On guard.
Feint 2 and cut 5.	Parry quarte (low), and (by dropping the point to the rear) cut 6 under the blade.
(Parry low tierce.)	
	On guard.
Feint 4 and cut 1.	Parry quarte and cut 4 under the blade.
(Parry seconde.)	
	On guard.
Feint 2 and cut 1.	Parry quarte, point in quarte.
(Parry quarte.)	
	On guard.

Reverse the lesson ; P. will commence.

Ripostes from the Tierce Parries.

M.	P.
Feint 1 and cut 2.	Parry tierce, cut 1 over the blade.
(Parry high prime.)	
	On guard.
Feint 4 (or 6) and cut 2.	Parry tierce, cut 4.
(Parry seconde.)	
	On guard.

Feint 5 and cut 2.	Parry tierce, cut 6.
(Parry tierce, low.)	

On guard.

Feint point in sixte and cut 6.	Parry tierce (low), cut 1 over the blade.
(Parry high prime.)	

On guard.

Feint 1 and cut 2.	Parry tierce, cut 5 under the blade.
(Parry quarte, low.)	

On guard.

Feint 1 and cut 2.	Parry tierce, point in tierce.
(Parry tierce.)	

On guard.

Reverse the lesson ; P. will commence.

Ripostes from Septime.

M.	P.
Feint 1 and cut 3.	Parry septime and cut 2 between his blade and his face.
(Parry high octave.)	

On guard.

Feint 2 and cut 3.	Parry septime and cut 4 by reversing the hand.
(Parry seconde.)	

On guard.

Feint point and cut 3.	Parry septime, point in quarte.
(Parry quarte.)	

On guard.

Reverse the lesson ; P. will commence.

Ripostes from Seconde.

M.	P.
Feint 1 and cut 4.	Parry seconde, cut 2.
(Parry tierce.)	

On guard.

| Feint 2 and cut 4. | Parry seconde, cut 1. |
| (Parry high prime.) | |

On guard.

| Feint 1 and cut 4. | Parry seconde, reverse the hand and cut 3. |

(Parry septime.)

On guard.

| Feint point in sixte and cut 4. | Parry seconde and point above the blade. |
| (Parry tierce.) | |

On guard.

Reverse the lesson ; P. will commence.

RIPOSTES FROM THE AUXILIARY PARRIES.

Ripostes from High Octave.

| Cut 2. | Parry high octave, cut 4. |
| (Parry seconde.) | |

On guard.

| Cut 2. | Parry high octave, cut 6. |
| (Parry tierce, low.) | |

On guard.

Reverse the lesson ; P. will commence.

Ripostes from the Prime Parries.

M.	P.
Cut 5.	Parry prime, cut 6.
(Parry tierce, low.)	

On guard.

Cut 5.   Parry prime, cut 4.
(Parry seconde.)

                        On guard.

Cut 5.   Parry prime, cut 1.
(Parry quarte.)

                        On guard.

Cut 5.   Parry prime, cut 5.
(Parry quarte, low.)

                        On guard.

Cut 5.   Parry prime, point.
(Parry quarte.)

                        On guard.

Reverse the lesson; P. will commence.

Ripostes from High Seconde.

        M.   P.

Cut 6.   Parry high seconde, cut 5
                                under the blade by re-
                                versing the hand.

(Parry quarte low.)

                        On guard.

Cut 6.   Parry high seconde, cut 2.
(Parry tierce.)

                        On guard.

Cut 6.   Parry high seconde, point.
(Parry tierce.)

                        On guard.

Reverse the lesson; P. will commence.

THE BEAT.

This is a forcible attack on the weapon, effected by striking aside the opponent's blade, in order to attack the opening thus formed; it may also be used as a feint.

It is executed as follows :—

M. and P. are engaged in the quarte medium. M. wishes to attack with cut 2 between his opponent's sword and his face ; he therefore turns his hand to tierce, strikes the foible of P.'s sword with the back of his own, and instantly delivers cut 2 at the right cheek.

The only defence for this is the high octave parry. Similarly, when engaged in the tierce medium, he will give the beat with the back of his sword in the form of sixte, and immediately deliver cut 1 at the left cheek. This attack will have to be parried with high prime.

Compound Ripostes.

These are nothing more than ripostes preceded by feints ; they are useful occasionally, but must be employed with much caution, as during the execution of them it is possible to be wounded by a remise.

The False Edge.

The attack with the false edge is usually directed against the sword-arm.

From the quarte medium.

M.	P.
Feint point at face and cut under the wrist with the false edge.	(Parry quarte, low.)

From the tierce medium.

Feint point at face and cut under the wrist with the false edge.	(Parry tierce, low.)

Against the high seconde guard.

Advance the point under the opponent's wrist and cut vertically upwards with the false edge.

Time Cut with False Edge.

M.	P.
Cut 4.	Slip the leg, raise the hilt, with the shell upwards, about as high as the head, and drop the false edge across the outside of the opponent's arm.

Combinations of Ripostes and Counter-Ripostes.

These exercises form a connecting link between the foregoing lessons and the assault; they consist of series of groups of attacks, parries, ripostes, and counter-ripostes, which I base upon the four principal parries—viz., quarte, tierce, septime, and seconde. I curtail them as much as possible, because they are intended mainly to serve as guides for instructors. A teacher who understands his business will be able to improvise lessons of this class according to the individual need of the pupil under tuition.

Series 1.—On the Quarte Parries.

M.	P.
1st.—Cut 1.	Parry quarte, cut 4.
Parry seconde, cut 2.	Parry tierce, cut 1 over.
(Parry high prime.)	
On guard.	

2nd.—Cut 1.   Parry quarte, cut 4.

     Parry seconde, cut 2.   Parry tierce, cut 5 under.

     (Parry quarte, low.)

                 On guard.

3rd.—Cut 5.   Parry quarte (low), point.

     Parry quarte, cut 2   Parry high octave, cut 4.
       over.

     (Parry seconde.)

                 On guard.

4th.—Cut 1.   Parry quarte, point.

     Parry quarte, cut 6.   Parry seconde, point over.

     (Parry prime.)

                 On guard.

Reverse the lessons ; P. will commence.

Series 2.—On the Tierce Parries.

1st.—Cut 2.   Parry tierce, cut 1 over.

     Parry high prime, cut 4.   Parry seconde, cut 2.

     (Parry tierce.)

                 On guard.

2nd.—Cut 2.   Parry tierce, cut 5 under.

     Parry quarte (low),   Parry quarte, cut 4.
       point.

     (Parry seconde.)

                 On guard.

3rd.—Cut 2.   Parry tierce, cut 5 under.

     Parry quarte (low),   Parry high octave, cut 6.
       cut 2 over.

     (Parry tierce, low.)

                 On guard.

4th.—Cut 6.   Parry tierce (low), point
                             over.

Parry tierce, cut 6.   Parry tierce (low), cut 1
over.

(Parry high prime.)
On guard.
Reverse the lessons; P. will commence.

Series 3.—*On Septime.*

1st.—Cut 3.   Parry septime, cut 4.
    Parry seconde, cut 2.   Parry tierce, cut 5 under.
    (Parry quarte, low.)
            On guard.
2nd.—Cut 3.
    Parry quarte, cut 2   Parry septime, point.
      over.   Parry high octave, cut 4.
    (Parry seconde.)
            On guard.
3rd.—Cut 3.   Parry septime, cut 2.
    Parry high octave,   Parry seconde, cut 2.
      cut 4.
    (Parry tierce.)
            On guard.
Reverse the lessons; P. will commence.

Series 4.—*On Seconde.*

M.   P.

1st.—Cut 4.   Parry seconde, cut 2.
    Parry tierce, cut 3.   Parry septime, point.
    (Parry quarte.)
            On guard.

2nd.—Cut 4.   Parry seconde, cut 1.
        Parry high prime, cut 5.   Parry quarte (low), cut 2
                                                       over.

    (Parry high octave.)
                        On guard.

3rd.—Cut 4.   Parry seconde, point over.
    Parry tierce, point   Parry seconde, cut 2.
        under.
    (Parry tierce.)

                        On guard.
Reverse the lessons ; P. will commence.

THE ASSAULT.

To Engage.

Having saluted, cross the blades and tap them smartly
together twice, then draw back the left foot so as to be out
of distance, and come to guard. Any hit given before this
is done is distinctly foul play.

A hit when received must be acknowledged frankly, and
it is as well further to follow the old custom of Mr. Angelo's
school by passing the weapon into the left hand, holding
the blade between the forefinger and thumb, about six
inches from the hilt, with the pummel to the front, extending the right arm with the hand open in supination.

If the sabres are very stiff the point must not be used, but
it should be permitted when they are light and pliable.

When leg-pads are not worn the Continental practice of
abstaining from cutting at the legs must be adhered to.
Similarly, when the singlestick is used, no inside cut must
be given below the line of the hip-joint. Such a cut is to
be considered foul play.

After making an attack, whether successful or not, recover at once to "guard," and in doing so shelter yourself under the "hanging guard," reverting afterwards to the medium.

When playing with a stranger avoid, if possible, being the first to attack, but endeavour to lead him on by showing openings, so that you may be able to study his style and temperament; receive his attacks with parry and riposte, and when he assails the low lines employ occasionally a stop-thrust or cut, supporting it by slipping the leg and drawing the haunches well back (*vide* Frontispiece). If he remains passive and shows wide openings regard them as a trap, against which feints must be employed to make him move his hand, and so discover his intentions.

Some fencers have a habit of stamping, shouting, etc., with a view to frighten their adversary; it is a foolish practice, by which very few people are affected at all, while in a case where the opponent has become momentarily abstracted the noise recalls him to his senses, when without it he might have been caught unawares.

When practicable attack direct; if you always employ a feint your opponent may perceive that, and time you while doing so.

Watch well the opponent's sword-hilt, observing his face also. The face is very often the index of the mind.

PART III.—THE BAYONET.

PART III.

THE BAYONET.

———◆———

THE weapon at present in use in our army possesses three factors of attack—namely, the point, which is of course the most important; the edges, which are mainly useful in riposte; and the butt, a knowledge of the use of which becomes under certain circumstances distinctly necessary.

It also presents three factors of defence,—the blade, which we must recognise as the foible, must naturally never be used for this purpose. The first, therefore, is the *forte*, or· that part of the stock which lies between the muzzle and the balance, with which most of the attacks of point are parried; the second is the *centre*, or the part between the balance and the small; and the third is the *butt*, which parries both thrusts and cuts directed at the lower lines.

THE GUARD.

The feet should now assume a position similar to that in the "guard" of foil and sabre play, with the exception that the left foot is in advance instead of the right. The body should be upright, but never stiff, and its weight equally distributed between the legs. The right hand, held a little in

advance of the right hip, should grasp the small of the butt;
while the left hand should hold the rifle at the balance, or,
if more convenient, an inch or two in front of it. The
weapon should rest easily in the hand, with the true (which
is the downward) edge in line with the centre knuckles
in a medium guard, not covering directly either inside or

Fig. 29.

outside, but ready to parry in any direction; it must be held
somewhat lightly, in order to avoid that rigidity of wrist and
arm which a tight grip invariably causes. The point must
be in line with the face of the opponent. When the
bayonets are engaged on the inside the guard will be a
quarte medium, and when on the outside a sixte medium.
(Fig. 29.)

The Resting Guard.

The object of this position is to afford repose to the limbs when the opponent is out of measure, in order that they may be thoroughly fresh for the assumption of active work when correct distance has been reached.

It is attained by drawing back the hands and lowering the rifle until the right hand rests on the upper part of the right thigh, and the back of the left hand and the wrist on the left thigh; the point is now directed a little low, and slightly off the line to the left.

The Voltes.

These movements are intended to effect a change of front in order to face a sudden flank attack; they are executed as follows :—

To the right, volte.—Turn to the right on the toes of the advanced foot, describing a quarter circle backwards from right to left with the rearward foot, which will bring it behind the other again to the position of "guard."

To the left, volte.—Turn to the left on the toes of the advanced foot, and, describing a quarter circle backwards from left to right with the rearward foot, bring it to the position of "guard."

When attacked from behind it is advisable to have recourse to the movement "about" in the bayonet exercise of Angelo : straighten the knees, and raise the musket to a perpendicular position, at the same time turn on the heels so that the right foot shall point to the proper rear and the left foot to the left, shifting the right hand to the balance and the left hand to the small, bend the knees, and bring the weapon down to the position of guard.

7

CHANGING GUARD.

Change Guard (from Right to Left) Retiring.

Turn on the toes of the right foot, using them as a pivot, and retire the left foot about two soles'-length behind it ; the right foot will now point to the front and the left foot to the left. At the same time extend the arms, with the rifle in a horizontal position, sufficiently to allow the heel-plate to. be quite clear of the body, and pass it across to the left side without shifting the hands, the right hand passing underneath the left forearm ; then seize the balance with the right hand and the small with the left. We are now in the position of " left guard."

Change Guard (from Right to Left) Retiring.

Turn on the toes of the left foot, and bring the right foot behind it, the left toe pointing to the front and right toe to the right ; extend the arms as before, and pass the rifle over to the right side, the left hand passing under the right forearm ; seize the balance with the left hand and the small with the right. We have now returned to the right guard.

Change Guard (from Right to Left) Advancing.

Turn on the toes of the left foot, bring the right foot forward in front of it, pass the rifle to the left as before, and come to left guard.

Change Guard (from Left to Right) Advancing.

Turn on the toes of the right foot, bring the left foot forward, pass the rifle across to the right, and come to right guard.

POINT PLAY.

It is imperative that these lessons should be given individually, and to that end the master should have the entire front of his body protected by a stout plastron.

In wielding the bayonet both hands should share in its manipulation, and neither hand should ever be used as

Fig. 30.

"lever" or "fulcrum." The four divisions of the body are similar to those recognised in foil play—namely, high inside or quarte line, high outside or sixte, low inside or septime, and low outside or seconde. The attack, except at a mounted man or at one running away, should never be made with a "lunge," owing to the loss of balance which with a hastate weapon the full lunge entails.

The Thrusts.

In bayonet fencing three modes of delivering the point are absolutely necessary,—the thrust, the throw, and the shorten arms,—as the following lesson will explain :—

On guard.—Fall back, by retiring the right foot, to the position of guard.

Fig. 31.

Prove distance.—Extend the rifle until the point touches the right breast of the master. On guard.

The weapons must now be crossed in the quarte medium, the point of juncture being just below the cross-guard.

Thrust.—Advance the rifle smartly in a horizontal position about the height of the right shoulder, barrel uppermost, to the fullest extent that the arms will allow, until the point strikes the breast of the master, at the same time completing the extension by bracing the right knee (Fig. 30).

On guard.—Withdraw the point and come to guard.

Throw.—Advance the point as before, *opening the advanced hand and allowing the rifle to glide over the palm of it* until the trigger guard (or magazine) comes in contact with it.

On guard.—Withdraw, etc.

The full throw in which the left hand quits the rifle altogether should only be used against a mounted or a retreating enemy, and then it must remain close to the weapon, so as to resume its hold the moment the thrust has been completed.

Shorten arms.—Bring the rifle down to a horizontal position with the point direct to the front, carry it back to the full reach of the arms and about level with the waist, the barrel resting on the left forearm : brace the left knee (Fig. 31).

Thrust.—Deliver the point as before.

The prime thrust may be used occasionally ; it is effected by raising the rifle, turning the sling uppermost till the back of the right hand is about as high as the ear, and delivering the thrust with the sling still up.

The change, disengagement, derobement, and cut over follow so distinctly the similar movements in foil play that it is needless to redescribe them.

PARRIES AGAINST POINT.

In bayonet fencing only simple parries can be used. They are four in number, protecting the four lines—namely, *quarte*, which defends the high inside ; *sixte*, for the high outside ; *septime*, for the low inside ; and *seconde*, for the low outside.

In all parries the attack must be received on the wood-

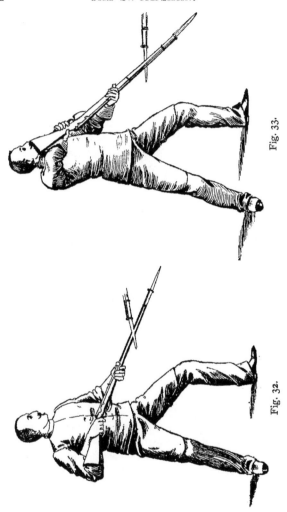

Fig. 33.

Fig. 32.

work of the rifle; and in their execution care must be taken to ensure the greatest possible flexibility, especially in regard to the arms and shoulders.

M. and P. will engage, crossing their weapons in the quarte medium.

M.	P.
Thrust.	Parry *quarte*, by passing the rifle slightly to the right, and so driving off the attack with the forte, while the point must be in no way deflected from the opponent's face.
	On guard.
Disengage and thrust.	Parry *sixte*, by turning the edge (causing the rifle to revolve in the advanced hand) just enough to allow the woodwork to meet the attacking weapon; make a light springy beat upon it near its point, and recover immediately from any deviation of the point from the direct line.
	On guard.
Derobe and thrust.	Parry *septime*, by lowering the point and passing the rifle slightly to the right, the point being still in line with the opponent (Fig. 32).
	On guard.

Engage in sixte medium.

Derobe and thrust.	Parry *seconde*, by lowering the point, turning the sling up, and making a slight beat on the enemy's weapon as in sixte (Fig. 33).

N.B.—The attacks on the low lines may also be very effectively parried by *under-sixte*,—of which more hereafter,—by raising the muzzle until the rifle is about perpendicular, and carrying off the advancing point by a vigorous sweep of the butt from right to left (see Fig. 35).

The above and all the ensuing lessons must be practised also from the left guard.

ADVANCED LESSONS.

Simple Attacks, Parries, and Ripostes.

When the pupil performs these lessons in a satisfactory manner they must be reversed.

Engage in quarte medium.

M.	P.
Thrust.	Parry quarte, derobe and thrust.
(Parry septime.)	
	On guard.
Derobe and thrust.	Parry septime, thrust high.
(Parry quarte.)	
	On guard.

Disengage and thrust. (Parry sixte.)

Parry sixte, thrust.

On guard.

Disengage and thrust.

Parry sixte, derobe and thrust low.

(Parry seconde.)

On guard.

Cut over and thrust.

Parry sixte, disengage and thrust.

(Parry quarte.)

On guard.

The above must also be performed from the sixte medium.

ATTACKS ON THE WEAPON.

Those most suitable to the bayonet are the pressure, the beat, and the froissement; they are effected in a manner similar to the same movements in foil play.

COMPOUND ATTACKS; OR, THRUSTS PRECEDED BY FEINTS, ETC.

These movements must be practised from both the quarte and the sixte medium.

Engage in quarte medium.

Feint a thrust and disengage.—Advance the point slightly, and as I parry quarte disengage to the opposite line and thrust.

Feint and derobe.—Feint as before, and on my parry of quarte drop the point to the lower line and thrust.

One, two (to deceive sixte).—Disengage, advancing the point a little, and on my parry of sixte disengage back again and thrust.

Under and over (to deceive septime).—Feint low, and on my parry of septime deliver the point high.

Thrust and one, two (to deceive quarte and sixte).—Feint thrust, I parry quarte, deceive by disengaging, I parry sixte, disengage again and thrust.

One, two, three (to deceive sixte and quarte).—Disengage, I parry sixte, disengage again, I parry quarte, deceive and thrust in sixte line.

Cut over and disengage (to deceive sixte).—Pass your bayonet over my point ; I parry sixte, disengage and thrust.

Cut over and derobe.—Cut over, I parry sixte, derobe and thrust at low line.

Cut over and one, two (to deceive sixte and quarte).—Cut over, I parry sixte, disengage, and I parry quarte, deceive it and thrust at sixte line.

The attacks on the blade may also be used as feints, as in foil play.

COMBINATIONS.

Engage in quarte medium.

M.	P.
Thrust.	Parry quarte, derobe and thrust.
Parry septime, thrust high.	Parry quarte, disengage and thrust.
(Parry sixte.)	

On guard.

Reverse the lesson.

Thrust low.	Parry septime, thrust high.
Parry quarte, disengage and thrust.	Parry sixte, derobe and thrust.
(Parry seconde.)	

On guard.

Reverse the lesson.

Disengage and throw.	Parry sixte and thrust.
Parry sixte, disengage and thrust.	Parry quarte, derobe and thrust.
(Parry septime.)	

On guard.

Reverse the lesson.

Press.	On the pressure derobe and thrust.
Parry septime and thrust high.	Parry quarte, disengage and thrust.
(Parry sixte.)	

On guard.

Reverse the lesson.

Froissé and throw.	Parry quarte, thrust low.
Parry septime, thrust high.	Parry quarte, disengage and thrust.
(Parry sixte.)	

On guard.

Reverse the lesson.

THE EDGES.

It is but seldom that a direct attack with the edge can be risked, and then only at the advanced hand, when the opponent's point is a little out of line ; but in riposte it is extremely useful when a carelessly executed parry on our part may have deflected on our point.

It must be observed that we have two edges,—the true edge, which is directed downwards, away from the muzzle ; and the false, which is directed upwards.

There are six cuts, three with the true and three with the false edge ; these cuts, when delivered, must be finished with a drawing motion to make the edge bite.

Cut 1 is given diagonally downwards, from right to left, at the left cheek or neck with the false edge.

Cut 2 is given diagonally downwards at the right cheek or neck, from left to right, with the true edge.

Cut 3 is given diagonally upwards, from right to left, at the sinews behind the advanced knee with the false edge.

Cut 4 is given diagonally upwards, from left to right, at the advanced knee with the true edge.

Cut 5 is directed vertically downwards at the advanced hand with the true edge.

Cut 6 is directed vertically upwards at the advanced hand with the false edge.

With a blade so short as ours, cuts at the body, which is often protected by thick clothing, are not to be recommended.

THE BUTT-THRUST.

Allow the bayonet to drop to the rear over the left shoulder, pass forward the right foot, and drive the heel-plate into the enemy's face.

THE BACK BUTT-THRUST

is useful when attacked very suddenly from behind; without moving the feet turn the body on the hips, and with the full swing of the arms force the heel-plate into the face of the assailant.

SUPPLEMENTARY PARRIES.

Cut 1, when delivered over the rifle as a riposte from quarte, must be parried with *prime*. Drop the point and raise the butt until the weapon is nearly vertical, but with the point a little forward, and turn the stock to the left front, allowing the rifle to revolve in the left hand; the right hand, which holds the small, must now be as high as the top of the head, so that you can look at the enemy underneath the wrist ; the left or advanced hand must be slided nearly to the muzzle, and the cut must be received on the centre, between the bands (Fig. 34).

Fig. 34.   Fig. 35.

Cut 2, when delivered over the rifle as a riposte from sixte, is even more difficult to stop than cut 1 ; it must be parried by *prime right* (high septime), by raising the rifle as in prime, but presenting the stock to the right front and receiving cut 2 on the centre.

Cut 3, which is delivered at the knee as a riposte after septime, must be parried with *under-sixte*.   Raise the point and drop the butt to the left front, shift the fingers of the right hand in such a manner that the small shall be momen-

Fig. 36.

tarily held between the thumb and the centre joint of the forefinger, and receive cut 3 on the butt ; it will be found that as the riposte is given the fingers will readily resume their normal position (Fig. 35).

Cut 4, delivered as a riposte after seconde, must be parried with *under-quarte*, manipulating the rifle as in under-sixte, but presenting the butt to the right front.

Cut 5 at the advanced hand can only be met by slipping the hand back and delivering a time-throw.

Cut 6 can either be parried with *horizontal quarte*, by bringing the rifle horizontally across the body, with the stock downwards, and receiving the cut on the centre (Fig. 36); or it can be avoided by slipping.

The butt-thrust should be parried with *horizontal prime*, by bringing the rifle horizontally across the body, stock upwards, with the bayonet pointing to the left, and forcing up the attacking butt until it is clear of the head (Fig. 36).

The parries of centre-sixte and centre-quarte are sometimes useful in a rally; they are formed with the point raised, the parry being effected with the centre.

COMBINATIONS OF THRUSTS AND CUTS.

Engage in quarte medium.

M.	P.
1. Thrust.	Parry quarte, cut 1 over the rifle.
Parry prime, thrust.	Parry seconde, cut 4.
(Parry under-quarte.)	

On guard.

Reverse the lesson.

2. Thrust.	Parry quarte, cut 1 over.
Parry prime, thrust prime.	Parry sixte (or centre-sixte), cut 2.
(Parry quarte.)	

On guard.

Reverse the lesson.

3. Disengage and thrust.   Parry sixte, cut 2 over.
   Parry prime right, thrust   Parry under-sixte, thrust
      low.   butt.

   (Avoid by slipping.)

                    On guard.

Reverse the lesson.

4. Derobe and thrust low.   Parry septime, cut 3.
   Parry under-sixte, cut 2.   Parry prime right, point low
                                  (sinking down to it).

   (Parry under-sixte.)

                    On guard.

Reverse the lesson.

BUTT FENCING.

Whether the encounter takes place in the fencing-room
or in the field, circumstances may, and often do, arise when
the combatants find themselves so close together that neither
dare withdraw nor attempt to disentangle himself, lest the
other should seize the opportunity to shorten arms and
deliver a fatal thrust; and it is in such cases that facility
in wielding the butt has to be recognised at its true value.

THE GUARD.

The combatants are *corps à corps*, with their rifles in
the quarte position and crossed at the centres (Fig. 37).

THE ATTACKS.

The attacks, in addition to the thrusts before described,
consist of four strokes, which must be effected with the

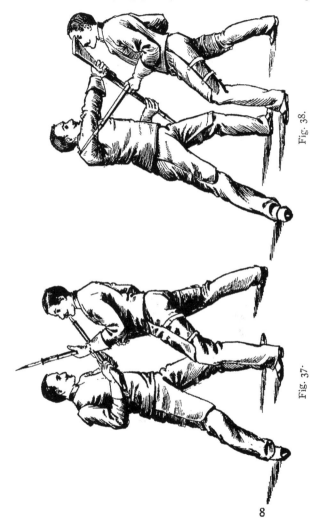

Fig. 38.

Fig. 37.

Fig. 40.

Fig. 39.

sharp projecting "toe." For use in the fencing-room the toe must be cut away, and the space filled in with curled hair and covered with leather.

The strokes must be directed, as openings occur, against parts only of the person upon which blows with an obtuse weapon will have serious effect.

Stroke 1. — Sink the point, raise the butt, and deliver the stroke over the rifle at the opponent's left cheek or temple (Fig. 38).

Stroke 2. — Raise the point till the rifle is very nearly vertical, and drive the "toe" home on to the points of the lower ribs (Fig. 39).

Stroke 3. — Pass forward the right foot and deliver the toe behind the left ear (Fig. 40).

Fig. 41.

Stroke 4.—Pass forward the right foot and deliver the toe against the lower part of the back in the region of the kidneys (Fig. 41).

THE PARRIES.

Stroke 1 must be parried by raising the butt, throwing the stock upwards in the form of *prime*, and receiving on the centre.

Fig. 42.

Stroke 2 must be parried with *horizontal quarte*, receiving on the centre.

Stroke 3 must be parried by raising the rifle to a vertical position in the form of sixte, with the left hand as high as and close to the left shoulder, receiving on the forte (Fig. 42).

Stroke 4 must be parried by raising the rifle as above, and receiving the stroke on the centre (Fig. 42).

COMBINATIONS OF STROKES.

M.	P.
1. Stroke 1.	Parry prime, stroke 2.
Parry horizontal quarte, stroke 1.	Parry prime.
	On guard.

Reverse the lesson.

2. Stroke 2.	Parry horizontal quarte, stroke 1.
Parry prime, stroke 2.	Parry horizontal quarte.
	On guard.

Reverse the lesson.

3. Stroke 3.	Parry sixte, stroke 2.
Parry horizontal quarte, stroke 1.	Parry prime.
	On guard.

Reverse the lesson.

4. Stroke 4.	Parry centre sixte, stroke 1.
Parry prime, stroke 2.	Parry horizontal quarte.
	On guard.

Reverse the lesson.

5. Thrust (butt).	Parry horizontal prime, stroke 2.
Parry horizontal quarte, stroke 1.	Parry prime.
	On guard.

Reverse the lesson.

THE ASSAULT.

The guard should be formed with the point a little more horizontal than it is in the lessons; but, excepting when engaged with a sabre, it should never be maintained in the low lines; such a position might attract a downward beat, which would be pretty certain to crush the barrel.

The combatants must be careful to preserve due elasticity of the limbs, and especially of the arms, which must be kept free from contact with any part of the person, except, of course, in the case of the resting guard.

When leg-pads are worn, hits should count as good ones on whatever part they may strike; but when these are dispensed with no hit must be allowed either at or below the knee.

A time-hit should only be counted as good where it saves the giver from being touched at all.

In point-play it is well to break the " rally " after three or four thrusts have been exchanged without effect, either by enclosing and coming to butt fencing or by springing back out of reach. Play with the bayonet very soon becomes disorganized.

The time at which the attack can best be made is when the enemy is meditating an attack himself, as he is sure to be off his guard.

RULES

1. THE platform or enclosure in which the contest takes place shall be at least twenty-four feet in length, and as nearly square as possible.

2. If a combatant allows himself to be *driven back* against the ropes, or in the case of a platform or its substitute, so that one of his feet should be off it, *a point must be scored to his opponent.*

3. The combatants must invariably engage out of measure.

4. The cuts and thrusts must not be given too heavily. Slogging does not constitute good play.

5. If a cut is made with such violence as to break down the parry it does not count as a hit.

6. In fencing with weapons pointed only no hit is a good one unless it would cause a punctured wound.

7. With the *sabre* or singlestick no cut is to be made inside lower than the hip-joint, unless suitable defensive armour is worn.

8. It is not permitted to parry any cut or thrust with the left hand, or to seize the opponent or his weapon with it.

9. In bayonet fencing strokes with the butt are allowable, but only when the butts are properly padded.

10. When a hit is effected, on whatever part it may be, the party receiving it must acknowlege it in a suitable manner. It is the business of the judges to decide as to its validity. Should he not acknowledge, but strike his opponent instead, *the blow is a foul one.*

11. When a hit is effected the *phrase d'armes* is concluded, and nothing further can be recognised until after the combatants have engaged anew.

12. If both combatants lunge and both hit, the hit shall count to neither.

13. If both hit at the same time, only one being on the lunge, the hit must count to the one who lunges.

14. A pass, in those exercises in which it is allowable, must be reckoned as a lunge.

15. With the *foil* the only hits which are valid are those which take effect on the *place d'armes* or target, which is on the breast, from the lower edge of the collar-bone to the waist, and is bounded vertically on the inside by a line passing over the left nipple, and on the outside by a line passing over the forward part of the armpit.

16. If two hits are given together, one on the lunge but not striking the *place d'armes*, and the other striking it but not on the lunge, the hit must count to neither combatant.

17. If a combatant *shifts his body* or shields himself with his arm or hand in such a manner as to protect the *place d'armes* from being touched, and receives a hit on the part so presented, such hit is to be counted a good one. If it is evident that he has resorted to such unfair tactics *for the purpose of balking* his opponent, he shall *also* forfeit a point from his score; and if the offence is repeated he *shall be disqualified.*

18. Should a combatant touch by a "remise," and at the same time be hit by the riposte of his opponent, the riposte is to count.

19. With the *fencing sword,* the play of which resembles an actual duel, all touches which would cause a punctured wound count as hits on whatever part they may strike; and if both of the combatants are touched, whether on the lunge or not, the hit counts to neither, as both would have been wounded.

20. *At the moment of engaging* the combatants must cross the points of their weapons, tapping them lightly together in order to show that both are ready. Any hit given before this is done is a *foul blow.*

21. In foil, sword, sabre, or stick play, any combatant *drawing back his arm* and stabbing as with a poniard shall forfeit a point for every such act; and if, after having been cautioned, he still persists therein he *shall be disqualified.*

22. No combatant is allowed to *shift his weapon* from one hand to the other, or in the case of bayonet fencing to "change guard" during an encounter; but he has the option of contending throughout it either as a right-handed or as a

left-handed man. Any blow given by such shifting of the weapon will be counted a *foul one.*

23. A combatant giving a *foul blow* shall have *one point for each foul blow deducted from his score ;* and if the offence is committed more than twice in the same bout (or heat), he must be disqualified from taking further part in the contest.

24. *If a combatant is disabled* or his play is in any way impeded by the injury caused by a *foul blow,* the party who has given it must be disqualified at once, as it is obviously wrong that he should be allowed to continue playing under an advantage resulting from his own brutality.

25. If one should disarm his opponent, or if the opponent should lose his weapon *by accident,* it is considered courteous to pick it up and return it to him.

26. If a combatant lose his weapon during a rally or *phrase d'armes,* and receive a hit *without any pause or interval of time,* such hit is a fair one ; if, however, a pause should occur after the loss of the weapon, *a hit then made is a foul one.*

27. A combatant *dropping his weapon* for—in the opinion of two out of the three judges—the purpose of avoiding being hit shall have a point deducted from his score for each such action ; and should this occur more than twice in the same bout *he must be disqualified for unfair play.*

28. In a competition nothing in the nature of a sword-knot must be allowed to be worn.

29. Any competitor making use of *outrageously rough play,* persistently *contravening the customary rules of fence,*

or adopting unfair tactics during a competition, shall be warned to desist therefrom ; and if, having been so warned, he still persists in such conduct he shall be *immediately disqualified*.

Judges.

To decide the issue of a contest there shall be three judges, who shall appoint one of their number president, and in him is vested the supreme control of the assault. They must all be swordsmen of known competency. Each judge should stand in such a position as to be able to watch one of the combatants, and as soon as that combatant receives a hit of any kind he must stop the combat in order to decide as to its validity ; and if there should be any difference of opinion regarding it, the decision of the president must be final.

The presence of the judges does not absolve the combatants from honourably acknowledging a hit when it has taken effect.

Either combatant perceiving that his opponent is guilty of a breach of the rules has a right to appeal to the president.

Copies of the rules should be hung up in conspicuous places in the fencing-room ; and in case of a contest for a prize it is advisable that a copy should be supplied to each competitor, as well as to the president and judges.

Judges should invariably insist on points and edges being coloured.

Handicapping.

In a competition it is sometimes necessary to handicap one of the combatants. The fairest way of effecting this is as follows :—Supposing A and B contesting a prize, the number of hits played for being 7, it is arranged that A shall give B 4 points ; B will, therefore, start at o, and will have to score his 7 hits, while A will start at minus 4, or 4 points behind o, which points he will have to make before commencing to score.

INDEX.

Printed by Hazell, Watson, & Viney, Ld., London and Aylesbury.

THE GRIPS AND CLOSES.

A DEFENCE AGAINST AN UNCIVILISED ENEMY.

THE GRIPS AND CLOSES.

A DEFENCE AGAINST AN UNCIVILISED ENEMY.

———◆———

To my mind the highest type of the barbarian fighting man
is the Afridi, armed with his *tulwar* or *chara*, and his round
shield. Now what will this Afridi do?—or rather, first
of all, what will he not do? He will not politely salute you,
he will not come on guard in correct fencing-room style and
abstain from attacking until the blades have been engaged,
and he will not in his fighting make use of the lunge and
recover to which we civilised swordsmen are accustomed,
for the very good reason that he knows nothing about these
things; but what he must and will do is exactly what
our English sword and buckler men did in the days of
Shakespeare, at which time the lunge had not been in-
vented. He will advance or retire, more or less quickly as
suits his purpose, with steps or "passes" as in walking or
running, he will "traverse" or move round you in a circle,
looking out for a chance to come in, or he will rush you
with a furious charge, his blows being mostly oblique downward strokes, and when attacked he will either parry with
his shield and strike at the same time, or he will "fly out,"
i.e., jump out of the way; and this is a style of fighting
to which we nineteenth-century fencers are not much

accustomed, so we must go back to our Elizabethan ancestors to find the best means of combating such tactics.

In those days there lived a sturdy English gentleman, George Silver by name, who devoted himself greatly to the study of arms, and who in 1599 published a curious little book which he called his "Paradoxes of Defence": it is in itself a work of small importance, but it serves as a kind of preface to a much more complete one which he afterwards wrote under the title of "Brief Instructions upon my Paradoxes of Defence for the True Handling of all Manner of Weapons." This book for some reason or another, possibly the death of the author, never came to be printed; it only exists in manuscript in the British Museum, where it was discovered by my late friend, Mr. William London, who made a complete *verbatim* and *litteratim* transcript of it, which, thanks to the kindness of his surviving relatives, is now in my possession. This "Brief Instructions" is to my mind the most valuable of all the ancient works of fence, for it gives us in the most clear and concise terms the exact method of fighting in use among our English ancestors. Silver uses in attack every part of the sword with which a blow can be given, even the pummel, a thing which lasted long after Silver's time; it is recommended by Lonnergan (1771), the typical master of the prize-fighting "gladiators" of the eighteenth century, who advises, "if the case requires the speedy chastisement of an insolent adversary, dart your pummel in his face, and trip his heels."

There is one other part of the weapon which our modern English sword instructors have lost sight of, and that is the "false" or back edge, and this "false" edge well sharpened may on occasion prove very useful, especially in dealing the terrible stroke known to students of old fence as the *coup de jarnac.* It is done this wise: having seized your opportunity, of which more anon, pass your point well behind the lower part of the advanced thigh of your enemy and then pull strongly, when your false edge will sever the great sinews of the ham and whatever else it may touch. A similar cut may be given in the high lines at the back part of the neck. Those old masters taught *fighting*, we teach nothing but *fencing* nowadays.

I propose now to show certain movements, tricks if you like to call them so, which, though scarcely admissible in fencing-room play, may mean the saving of a man's life when fighting in grim earnest, especially when opposed to such a rough customer as our typical Afridi.

It is from George Silver that I intend mostly to borrow, who devotes an entire chapter to " The manner of certain gryps and clozes to be used at the syngle *short* sword fyght," etc. : the "cloze" means the inevitable *corps à corps* which must result from the furious rush of the enemy, and the " gryp " means, after having parried his cut, the seizing of his sword hand with your own left, followed by actions which I shall presently describe. These things are extremely simple, and may be used with advantage by a resolute man, although he may not be a very brilliant swordsman according to our modern notions.

The grips, etc., are to be effected as follows :—

GRIP I.

The enemy charges you with an oblique downward cut at your left shoulder.

Parry high prime. Advance your left foot, and pass your left hand, the thumb being downwards, and the back of your hand to your right, under your own sword and seize his sword hand or wrist, forcing it downwards and drawing it in towards your left side.

9

Actions of the sword :—

- (*a*) Very promptly deal him a strong blow on the right side of his head with your pummel.
- (*b*) Throw back your right shoulder so as to prevent his seizing your sword arm, and give him a thrust or cut in the high lines, or, if his lower parts are more open, the *coup de jarnac* will be found very effective.

GRIP II.

On the same attack parry quarte, step in and seize his wrist underneath, forcing it a little upwards to your own left.

Actions of the sword :—

- (*a*) Drop the point of the sword to the rear over your left shoulder, and give him the pummel on his forehead.
- (*b*) Draw back your right shoulder to prevent his gripping you, and use your point or edge where he is most open.
- (*c*) Pass your point over his left shoulder in such a way that the blade shall be in a transverse position behind him with the false edge against the back of his neck, and draw your sword strongly towards you.

GRIP III.

The enemy charges you with an oblique downward cut at your right shoulder.

Parry tierce. Pass forward your left foot, seize his hilt or wrist with your left hand and force his sword arm upwards towards your own right, thus deviating his shield from the line of defence.

Actions of the sword :—

- (*a*) Thrust or cut him, not forgetting your *coup de jarnac*, where he is most open, which will be underneath.
- (*b*) Having seized him as above, force his hand downwards to your right, and thrust or cut him in the upper lines.
- (*c*) Having seized him as above, force his sword hand to your own left, and, acting as after the quarte parry and seizure, cut, thrust, or give the pummel as may be convenient. Should he drop his shield and come in to grapple with you, then quickly pass your sword behind your back, leaning your wrist against your left side, and present your point at his belly.

GRIP IV.

Your enemy charges you and cuts low at the left side, leg, or fork.

(*a*) Parry septime, seize his wrist from above, carrying his sword hand to your left, and cut or thrust him as is most convenient.

(*b*) Parry low prime, seize from above, and strike him an upward blow with your *pummel underneath* his chin.

An attack in the low line on the right is to be parried with "seconde" and answered with a riposte; gripping is unadvisable here, as it tends to upset your own equilibrium. Silver gives a particularly wise piece of advice about these seizures, which I will repeat in his own quaint words :—
" Do you never attempt to cloze or com to your gryp at these weapons, unless it be at the slow motion or disorder of your enemye, but if he will cloze with you then you may

safely take the grype of him at his comynge in." In plain English these grips are to be regarded solely as an extra means of defence.

I cannot help thinking that to those whose conditions of service imposes on them the probability of meeting with warriors of the barbarian type a certain knowledge of wrestling would be useful—a man in Silver's time was hardly looked upon as a complete swordsman without it. A vast amount of fuss is made in the Army nowadays about boxing, but wrestling appears to have been entirely ignored.

Printed in Great Britain
by Amazon

52912342R00083